What people are saying about
Signals From The Child

"Jean Coles has given us a window to the souls of our children. In my 23 years as a counselor I have found children's drawings essential in performing psychological evaluation, and have often used the information providing expert testimony in court for abused children. I wish this book had been available years ago, as it is a wealth of information in a very readable and thoughtful resource.

Anyone who works with children or who lives with them would find this a treasure of a book in helping to better understand these complicated little people and the images they make."

Deborah McKenna, M.A., L.P.C.

"How do you communicate with a three-year-old who has just been uprooted from one country to another? Or a youngster starting another new school who won't speak about his feelings but spends endless hours drawing?

Jean Coles, author of *Signals from the Child*, offers both guidance and reassurance to relocating parents including that old maxim: sometimes a drawing is just a drawing."

Robin Pascoe, Relocation Author, ExpatExpert.com

"In the thirty years I have been in the classroom, I have seen the importance of children's art. This book is just what I need.

Signals from the Child, an informative resource and a fascinating read, has given me new ideas regarding how to look at the art created as children express their feelings and needs.

I look forward to using this information when dealing with students and teachers, as well as parents."

Lynnette Disheroon, AAECE, AACD, Head Teacher,
Kempe Children's Center
University of Colorado
Health Sciences Center
Department of Pediatrics

Signals
From The
Child

*Learn to Read the Secrets in Drawings
and Refrigerator Art*

Jean Coles

HOUSE

**P.O. Box 100891
Denver, CO 80250
800-690-EMBA (3622)
www.signalsfromthechild.com**

Signals From The Child: Learn to Read the Secrets in Drawings and Refrigerator Art.
Copyright © 2003 Jean Coles
First Printing 2003

Library of Congress Control Number: 2002096851

Family/Psychology
Includes bibliographical references and index
ISBN 0-9723529-2-9

Disclaimer

This book is designed to provide information on the drawings of average children, to include teens, and not intended to provide therapy for the parent or child. It is sold with the understanding that neither the publisher nor the author is engaged in rendering legal, psychological nor any other professional service. If assistance is required the reader should consult with licensed or certified professionals. All effort is made to make this book as accurate and complete as possible, however it should be used only as a guide. There could be inaccuracies or misunderstandings. The reader must assume responsibility for his or her own interpretation of a drawing. It is not the intent of this book to include all opinions or information available through other sources. Read others for additional interpretations. See the appendix for a starting place. The purpose of this manual is to entertain and inform. Neither the author nor the publisher shall have liability nor responsibility to any person or entity for any loss or damage alleged to have come from relying on the information contained in this book.

Bulk purchases of this book for reselling, incentives, gifts or fund raising are available. Please contact the publisher for quantity discounts.

My Special Thanks

With gratitude to my husband Stuart, who routinely makes few demands on my time, while providing his endless support for this venture

To those who read, suggested, and encouraged with so much enthusiasm, Vickie Miller, Jeannie Stephens, Dana Stephens, Pat Kaspar Coles and Rose Kuszmaul among them. Special thanks to Jeannie and Pat for unique exemplars

To David R. Coles, who has brought both awe and terror to generations of high school students; he willingly picked nits, captured wandering participles, and continues to rail at the incomplete sentence

Gratitude and devotion to Kyle Stephens, who can do practically anything with a computer

To Val Sagrillo who brought her talent and patience to make my vision of the cover materialize

To Sister Veronica Ruskamp, Master Graphoanalyst, for her early expression of excitement regarding my subject

To instructors Joan Cook and Nadelle Claypoole, for erasing the imaginary boundaries of graphology

With appreciation to the family of Rachel Scott for their time talking with me, and the sharing of her drawing

And finally, to Bernie S. Siegel, MD., one of the few pioneers in the field of therapeutic drawings for decades, for his generosity and support when he learned of my project.

Dedicated
to grandparents everywhere,
slightly weighted to grandmothers,
because of my own.

Preface...a note to the reader

You may have picked up *Signals from the Child* in curiosity and then decided you had never seen a book like it. My experience was the opposite. Once my interest was piqued I was unable to find this information in one practical form for the layperson. Yet, I have not regretted in any way the delightful exploration of the many authorities and many aspects of the same issue.

Numerous books by artists and art therapists, teachers, physicians, graphologists, psychologists and psychiatrists, as well as those who specialize in symbols are listed in the bibliography. I recommend that you continue reading further. Many of the books are hard to find, and do remember please, that academics write for each other.

Which of us hasn't paused over a drawing that a child has proudly conjured for us, or wondered at a squiggle we have made in the margin of a notepad. My fascination with the marks we leave on paper led me to study graphology and become certified in graphoanalysis almost two decades ago.

Symbols have drifted throughout the civilized past into the mainstream of daily life through art, religion and literature and we acknowledge their presence in many forms. If you happen to be a person of common sense and somewhat trusting of your intuitive nature this information will all fall into place easily. And you will have the greatest advantage— that of knowing the nature and situation of the drawer of the pictures you will gradually learn to interpret. There is no voodoo involved.

Now *you* can glimpse what was on the mind *at the time* the image was sketched. It serves us well to remember that these kiddos can draw something entirely unrelated in the next impulse.

For teachers, parents and grandparents the knowledge here can be invaluable. For any of us it is, at the very least, interesting. My one small regret? That I didn't have this information when my children were small.

Have fun with this.

Jean Coles, CGA

Contents

Drawings are untitled, explained by the surrounding text, and
are numbered consecutively throughout the chapters.

Introduction

Researching children's drawings brings one into contact with many disciplines. It is important for the nonprofessional to stay constantly aware that he or she is not a therapist. To counsel another in any way requires licensing and certification, and even then one is wise to depend upon a therapist with extended experience as well as recognized credentials.

The flip side of this issue is the fact that those with the capacity and the diligence to pursue a PhD are not automatically also gifted as art therapists. Certainly talented psychiatrists over the years have contributed the bulk of the testing and case history conclusions.

You won't find any quizzes or case presentations in these pages, only a cross section of exemplars accumulated over the years and drawings specifically sketched for illustration. Those reproduced from any other source will be identified.

The drawings are in black and white in order to study the content. Are colors important? They can be vital in healing therapy, but do leave this to the professional. I'll point out in these drawings where color makes a difference.

Art therapy is a fascinating field, peopled with wonderfully dedicated folks, who have the skill and patience to guide others, often children, through artistic expression to a desired understanding or conclusion. As a combination of art and psychology it allows communication in a natural, visual way when it might be impossible with words. Many forms are used—crayons, pencils, pens, paint, clay, collage and even sand sculpture—to aid communication. Many also utilize "cooperative drawings" with family members and in marriage counseling. The art therapy discipline requires the active participation of the therapist and individual clients.

Bernie S. Siegel, M.D., the renown cancer surgeon who wrote *Love, Medicine & Miracles* considers drawings from the patient crucial to the prognosis. He states that "Such drawings bypass verbal deceptions and get to the universal symbolic language of the unconscious."

One of the most knowledgeable approaches to the language of drawing that I've seen, whether by her instinct or intention, is that of Dr. Betty Edwards, Professor of Art at California State University, Long Beach. Part II of her book *Drawing on the Artist Within* is an excellent source in understanding how emotion can be conveyed to paper. I don't know that she has had any exposure to graphology but she certainly "gets it." Her work with what she calls "analog drawings" goes to the core of this exciting work.

Graphology is the obvious foundation for analysis of drawings, especially in the use of the page itself and the application of the drawing tool, all of which will be covered in the first section.

It was a struggle to have graphology reclassified from hobby to the status of professional occupation, but the U.S. Department of Labor did just that in 1990. This occurred a full decade after it was reassigned to the psychology section in the Library of Congress.

Europe has always been ahead of the United States in the understanding of and respect for graphology, perhaps because of its origins there.

Pick up any book of symbols and you may well lose an hour or two before your nose comes out of the fascinating material you will find.

I trust you will have a similar experience here, with an ability to see and read what you have only been looking at casually under the refrigerator magnet.

In much of the material I've researched there is a tendency of the analyst to decipher what the drawing indicates, but not tell the reader how to decode it. On occasion, I've seen a dreadful, subjective interpretation trying to prove the analyst's point of view. Keep an objective eye and attitude, weigh one piece of information against another, and remember that in one drawing we see a reflection of the feelings of the artist, not the whole person.

Signals from the Child is a compendium of professionally accepted and recognized symbols in children's art, but certainly not *every* opinion in the field. Should I offer my own opinions, they'll be identified at the time.

Chapter One
Begin At The Beginning

"Drawing is the art of taking a line for a walk."
Paul Klee

The only complicated part of our adventure in these pages will be proceeding step by step, so follow your inclination right now and flip through the entire book. Read the introduction please, and come right back.

No matter how intriguing you find the drawings and definitions you will need a grounding in how to approach an artwork and this is *the* chapter. You will learn how the placement of the drawing on the page affects the interpretation of it, and how the tool can reflect the feelings of the artist. You will understand pressure, and learn to recognize where a stroke begins and ends.

A friend of mine, a middle-aged salesman, noticed my busy work of collecting samples from acquaintances. He drew one for me and stared at me for a minute, then asked "what does it mean when a little boy draws airplanes and guns and bombs falling?" I answered, "it usually means that he's a little boy." He stared at me again then walked away smiling, saying, "I'm really glad you said that "

One of the primary things to accept is that often a drawing is just a drawing.

Drawing...What drawing?

To date, the drawings I collect are spontaneous, rather than any sort of a guided sketch. An art therapist or a psychiatrist will sit with a client/patient and discuss what is being done on the page. I feel it is important not to do this, but to instead expect the child to present you with an arbitrary picture of his own creation. You can of course, utilize the age old "tell me about this figure" or "what does this mean to you?" when it is completed. Many times you fall heir to a fascinating drawing with no artist to explain it. Be careful in this instance not to leap to a conclusion.

I collect tree drawings. On occasion an adult or a child will draw one in my presence. Over the years I've evolved a way of placing the paper askew on the table rather than handing them a sheet. Can you guess why?

A sheet of unlined paper is treated a lot like a dinner plate. Most of us will adjust it and rearrange it at our place setting. There is a slight chance that someone can accept an 8½ x 11 paper and feel he must use it as it was given to him. With a tree drawing especially, it makes a difference which way the paper is turned.

So I put a few sheets of unlined paper in a random stack on the table, let the artist select the pencil, pen or marker for the drawing and find something else to do until he is finished.

I offer a variety of implements simply by the handful on the table or from a pencil holder. People are particular about the instrument they use, especially adults. Have you noticed your own preference? Some simply cannot write with a different line width pen or pencil than they are used to. And yes, it "means something."

Selecting The Tool

Age will dictate the instrument for the picture early on, but as the child comes into his own he may show a preference for colored pencil or ballpoint over markers.

The narrow markers are usually handled well, but avoid the bulky wide markers, as they are often not used in a natural way.

For our purposes, the pencil (colored or #2 lead), the ballpoint pen, or the crayon is ideal for judging the pressure used in the drawing.

Pressure

One of the surest ways to check the temperament of an individual is to note the sort of implement used to write or draw and how heavily the mark is made.

Pressure can be felt through the paper between your thumb and forefinger if you have an original drawing.

To simplify for our purposes here, the thicker the point of the tool, the heavier the mark left on the paper, the more intense the energy of the drawer. This can vary by mood to some small degree but routinely even children have a preference for the kind of writing tool and how they use it.

By the time one reaches adulthood the taste is well defined. My husband for instance, simply cannot make a note in hurry with a fine-line pen. Expecting him to sign his signature with anything other than a heavy roller ball is futile. The fine-line writer, who uses light pressure, *can* adapt more easily for the moment but still feels fraudulent using a pen with a thick point.

Those who use heavy pressure have a vitality about them and give all of their energy to the activity of the moment. They tend to be strong-willed, tenacious and excitable but can also be inspirational to others.

Folks using a medium pressure have a healthy willpower and are adaptable. They concentrate their energy where and when it is needed.

If the pressure is light and "skipped" the personality is overly sensitive and impressionable. There may be a lack of commitment and energy. These folks are tolerant, sometimes to a fault.

Average pressure is not heavily "embossed" or carried through to the back of the paper, so if you examine a normal pressure drawing with heavy pressure and embossing in a certain area give it your full attention. The area involved will betray some anxiety or if supported by other clues, even announce anger.

We have to judge reproduced lines by the appearance on the page. In most cases pressure can be visible.

Figure 1

You can see the different pressure in these marks as well as the change in pressure on some of the lines. All were made with the same pencil.

Strokes

The pressure will change from the point we start the tool on the paper, leaving a dark stroke and sometimes a dot, to a feathering where we end the stroke. Often the ballpoint pen will also leave a dot where the direction changes. Why do you need to know this? It can serve you well in analyzing an abstract drawing to see what starts where, and in seeing strokes that are added to others in any drawing. Often it is valuable to see the direction the stroke is headed or where it begins and ends. You'll see more as we go further along.

Figure 2

It should be apparent which set of strokes started at the bottom and which at the top. In figure 3 one set starts from the left, the other from the right. Notice how unnatural it is for a right-handed person who did this example, to stroke from right to left.

Figure 3

The upstroke in drawing and handwriting is lighter than the downstroke. This relates to pressure. It takes more effort to bring the stroke down than to lift it. See the difference in figure 4? Should you ever have a drawing, whether an abstract or a scribble, you can always tell up from down with this information.

Figure 4

Test yourself in figure 5. Where does the star begin and end? How many separate strokes in the square?

Figure 5

The star begins with a firm upstroke at the lower left, comes straight down, up to the left, straight over to the right and down to the left ending in a feathery stroke beyond where it began. The square has three strokes. The left side is straight down, one more goes across the top to the right and down without lifting the tool. The last goes across the bottom and crosses the right side.

Figure 6

Well, what have we here in figure 6? Perhaps a budding author. This kindergarten girl is desperate to learn to write script. Her effort is more than good, and this excerpt gives us a chance to confirm our information regarding the up and down pressure. A tip from graphology—keep a magnifier handy for these excursions.

This lovely "sun" in figure 7 done by an 8 year-old gives us a fine example of pressure and directional strokes.

Figure 7

She may have moved the paper as she added the rays and notice how slowly the circle was drawn trying to keep it as round as possible. Objects completed quickly do not have repetitions or a wobbling line.

Really good graphologists get a chuckle out of those enthusiastic souls who try to analyze every blip or hiccup in a sample. Some folks, after all, have been known to lay the paper over crumbs on the table and continue writing!

Placement On The Paper

Now that you understand strokes and pressure, let's find out why it makes a difference where they are drawn on the paper, regardless of the size of the page.

The diagram you see in figure 8 is more than adequate for interpreting a child's sketch. It is only basic for an adult effort.

A drawing will often have a direction or a slant to it. Refer back to figure 5. See how both objects list to the right? The movement can also be interpreted in the same way. An object such as a tree or a house started in the middle can take a left or right direction.

The diagram (I dislike the word "schema" for unknown reasons) in figure 8 is easily read and you might want to mark the page and refer to it. It only *appears* ominous.

There are no borderlines to define *exact* areas, other than a definite division from top to bottom in the middle of the sketch. The left is all things female, to include attitude as well as relatives and obviously, the mother figure. It can reflect a preoccupation with the past. The right reflects all things masculine, to include attitude, relatives and the father figure. There may be strong interest in future events and projects.

Be clear on these points. The boy drawing on the left side or to the left may be influenced by females or may be a passive person. In no way does it color his masculinity. The girl with tendencies toward the right may have unusual drive or be devoted to the father. Her femininity is intact.

An easy way to remember the influence of the page is to consider the top third to be the domain of thought. The middle section of the page relates to action, such as the way we interact with those around us. And in the bottom one third of the paper our instincts and base emotions reside.

Again remember, these are vague borderlines. Young artists use the bottom of the page. Why? They react to most situations emotionally and instinctively. As they learn social skills they will draw in the center portion or incorporate the space into their work. Then as they develop their mental skills they find a way to use the top of the page. The young child who draws at the top of the paper rather than elsewhere is a crackerjack!

Aspiration
Idealism
Enthusiasm
Ambition

Past	Present	Future
Feminine	Sociability	Masculine
The Mother	Self Esteem	The Father
Passivity	Expression	Activity

Physicality
Practicality
Unconscious
Instincts

Figure 8

Here we see in figure 9 the sketch of a 5 year-old boy who was given a class assignment to draw "rain." He is the kind of crackerjack we're talking about. He draws black clouds and blue rain but he's positioned himself on the top of the mountains *at the top of the page.* An assignment of rain doesn't dampen his enthusiasm. He uses bright colors for the mountains and has a rainbow in the center under the cloud. We'll get to the "sun" hands in a later chapter.

Figure 9

Because I don't like assigned pictures for our purposes, I will always identify them for you and there won't be many. These two that I've selected, however, are perfect to recognize enthusiasm. What better vehicle than rain, which carries the stigma of depression, to show how the happiness in the child will burst through.

In figure 10 a 5 year-old girl in the same class becomes a joyful participant in the rain. She floats as high as the tree under a rainbow-colored umbrella.

Figure 10

Her colors are natural. The tree has a brown trunk, green crown and the ground (grass) is green. She's given herself a bright red dress and hair. She enjoys the pretty blue raindrops, as she probably does in life also.

Position Of The Paper

As I mentioned earlier, the way the drawer chooses to position the sheet of paper will give her space either vertically or horizontally. Don't pay much attention unless she draws very little in the picture. Primarily it is a question of whether she has a landscape in mind or an object that requires height. "So...?" you're saying.

Unless otherwise labeled, the sketch of a person of the same sex and age as the artist, represents the artist herself. When you find little else in the picture and the drawing is on the horizontal axis and contains either of these elements, assume that the child is expressing a dominance of her space. She feels entitled to more latitude than other playmates. She might be controlling of those around her, even somewhat conceited. If you know the subject and she is none of these, then we must consider the rare alternative interpretation, which is a strong tendency to escape into a fantasy world, usually for emotional reasons.

Paper width of 12 inches. Top 2/3 cropped.

Figure 11

Paper width of 11 inches. Top 2/3 cropped.

Figure 12

Your Approach To An Interpretation

Many professionals have put their reputations on the line, especially in the last seventy years, to develop, analyze, and record these interpretations. We are obligated to convey their findings in a conservative and thoughtful manner. We are not crystal-gazing or reading chicken bones here.

I have run across fascinating drawings that cannot be unlocked without knowing what inspired them. I refuse to guess, and you must also.

Your initial inclination will be to glance at a sketch and start interpreting. If you have children or grandchildren the urge will be almost irresistible. Don't. The one reliable thing you can do is to see how it feels to you. Then put it in a spot where you will see it often for a few days. All together now...how about "the refrigerator!"

When I am concentrating on a drawing, I place it on a wallboard in my office. I leave it there until it "speaks" to me. You too, will be amazed at the things you'll see if you give it time to percolate.

Notice the use of the space, the energy of the pressure...is it drawn heavier in a particular location? Give it your attention. If it is a group picture pay attention to who is standing by whom. Notice who is omitted, if anyone, from a family drawing. If the drawing has people separated notice what object, if any, is in between.

The drawings here have been left with as much detail as possible, warts and all. You may see extraneous marks, dots or smearing present in the sketch. Retouching can rob important detail. Neatness or carelessness tells you about the child. This information is important to your analysis.

If you notice yourself finding phallic references all over or negativity about one area consistently, stop and consider yourself. Are you inserting your experiences into the interpretation? Back away and take a peek at the baggage you are carrying. Be really honest with each sample.

For instance, if you are a grandmother and don't like the stepfather, use extra caution in trying to interpret a grandchild's recent treasure of refrigerator art.

Never offer an interpretation from something a person hands you, saying "what does this mean?" Do it your way, the responsible way.

And again...sometimes a drawing is just a drawing.

ChapterTwo
Expectation Of Ages One To Five

The progression of drawings we'll be covering relate more to stages, and references to age are general. Don't try to read anything in, regarding intelligence, when a child is in one stage for a longer period. Early analysts tied the drawing to brain-power, but my, how we've progressed. There are so many things to influence a child. Don't discount hand-eye coordination and the child's preference for a style.

Age One and a Half to Two

When a child is given a crayon and paper a brand new world opens for him, and for mom also if she doesn't monitor his drawing surface carefully. Scribbling is one of the first stages in the development of hand-eye coordination, and some say one of the best, for developing reading skills.

Analysts have various meanings for scribbles (as well as many other things in this field). Some analyze them in depth, others will pass over them quickly.

Figure 13

I suggest that you measure them by pressure and intensity and you may find even these will change regularly. Otherwise, I feel that a child's scribbling is exploration until the time he can talk. To learn more about scribbling "styles," consult Rhoda Kellogg's books listed in the bibliography.

We adults, especially those who hover over a tot, will begin asking the meaning. "Is this a picture of the dog?" "Can you draw Mommy?" "Tell me about your picture." Thus the child learns connections between his masterpiece and the world around him.

As a young mother I can remember my kids trying to answer my questions after they finally got my attention to look at yet another scribble. None of this held interest for me yet. "Tell me about your picture." (yawn) "It's a puppy running," she said. (Maybe my daughter is a genius, I thought, hopefully.) "It's a helicopter," my son explained. (He's not destined as an artist, but what a sweet kid.)

When I found out, many years later, how we should interpret these explanations it was a head-slapper for me! The little artist is using the tool *as* the puppy or the helicopter and the marks on the paper are merely the tracking of the imagined movement. Mom had been invited to the party but she didn't show up.

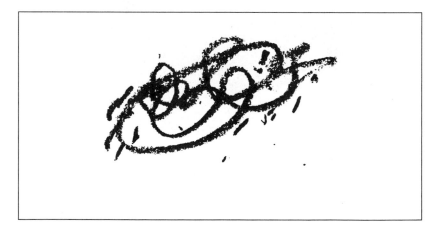

Figure 14

Scribbling at age 1¹/₂ to 2 may have no real intention but we can see that it launches the little artist by developing control. As we progress through the stages try to capture your own first memory of drawing and see if you can relate to feelings at the time. Mostly we cannot, but what a reference for you, especially if you have saved your own drawings. This could provide a wonderful starting place for you, especially if you remember the circumstances.

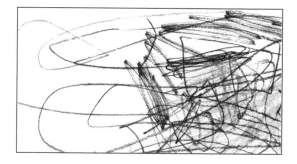

Figure 15

Figure 16

Thanks to a Special Lady

One of the most prominent sources in the knowledge of young children's drawings is Rhoda Kellogg. I had the good fortune to discover her work early on.

A nursery-school teacher in San Francisco, she was self-taught and for years the object of much derision. She doesn't mince words in her books, nor suffer fools.

As the interest in child art by psychologists grew, she openly stated that they had seen and studied so few *normal* children's drawings that they had to settle for the Draw-A-Man test and apply their various psychological theories of child behavior to explain it. Her opinion of the Draw-A-Man test from her book, *Children's Drawings Children's Minds*: "Pure commercial hogwash."

She saved and methodically cataloged over a *half-million* drawings from all over the world. She gained well-deserved recognition later in life. Educators and students, as well as rival therapists and psychologists, study at the library she launched in San Francisco, The Rhoda Kellogg Child Art Collection of the Golden Gate Kindergarten Association.

Kellogg seems to have proven that children from all over the world follow a general pattern of graphic development. Scribbles lead to lines and basic forms, including the circle to form the mandala motif.

Mandala means "magic circle" or "sacred circle" in Sanskrit. Swiss psychiatrist Carl Jung adopted the word for the drawings of his patients and associated the mandala with the Self, the center of our being.

Soon the circle form grows "legs" and becomes the "tadpole" form. This form evolves into many similar shapes and gradually to those representing the human form, more or less. Not all children use every shape.

She stresses the gap between the acrobatic mind of a normal child and the analysis of the adult professional, who is often trying to label the child.

Kellogg doesn't provide a lot of analysis, however anything you care to learn about children's art development by age is there, in mind-boggling abundance.

You know those tiresome questions such as "what person, alive or dead, would you most like to have dinner with?" Rhoda Kellogg would rank high on my list.

Age Three

There is a tendency for children at this time to pick up on things in their environment while they are busily engaging the rules in this thing called life. There is scribbling, of course, but it will be combined with other shapes that may be identified as a person or an object one minute and something completely different the next.

The scribbles are evolving into more concentrated productions involving circles, squares, crosses and lines, commonly referred to as geometric forms.

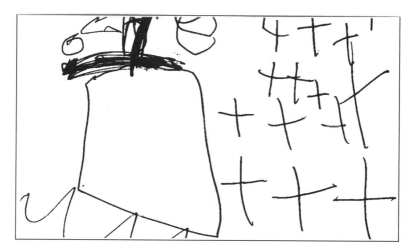

Figure 17

Figure 18

The mandala shape makes its appearance often, sometimes with a design inside such as in figure 19.

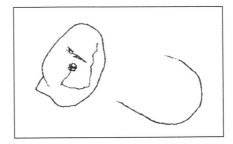

Figure 19

Other times the addition is on the outside of the circle, usually in the form of "rays". You may find a combination, such as in figure 20.

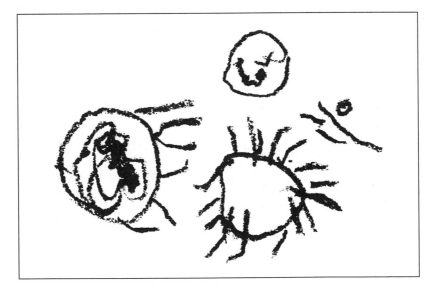

Figure 20

At some time during this year the child will start adding "legs" and what we recognize as a "face" rather than a design, as in figure 21, becoming what is known as the "tadpole" human.

Figure 21

The "tadpole" humanoid will continue evolving with the addition of various forms of facial features, along with what adults call "arms" attached to the "head"...or is it the "body"?

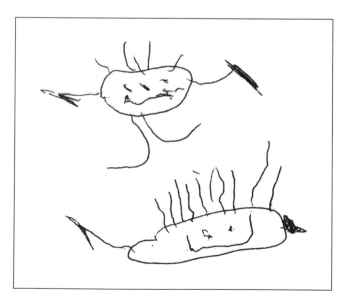

Figure 22

Figure 23

All tadpole humanoids are normal for this age and even beyond, as the child exercises the drawing muscles for the big job yet to come, that of drawing the human and other basic forms.

Do remember the ages are approximate and the child may continue with a form of choice even after discovering a new one.

Age Four

Prepare for an abundance of pictures, many of them with charming renditions of the human form. You may also find some of questionable derivation. Unable to identify them with full confidence as human, just accept them as critters.

Figure 24

Personally, I find this riotously cute, as I also do figure 25. It was done in purple marker. When I looked at it, I knew it was a 4 year-old but was surprised to find it was drawn by a girl. (It's good to be kept humble.)

The head treatment may be hair, a crown or judging by the figure, even spines. At this age, the head treatment is included in some drawings and not in others.

The legs have been blessed with "feet" but there are no hands. The arms and legs spring from the head and there is scribbling and "free-form" present. Children this age and beyond are not trying for realism and are content without it.

In figure 25 we have yet another expression. This boy (I was correct this time) has added a body to the mandala head, and I suspect those lines under it are legs.

Figure 25

What's that you say? The hands? Ah, you noticed. Before we go there, take a peek at the shoulder area. I've no doubt in examining pressure, that he took a look at those heavy hands and decided he needed something to hold them up. He added the horizontal lines, did a bit of erasing to get it right and added the "muscles." This is advanced for a 4 year-old child.

The hand on your right is a common display of a "sun-hand." It emerges this year and may be drawn for many more. It has no particular meaning except to adults who think the child is trying to draw a real one. We have another mandala formation.

The claw-like hand may be pure whimsy and fun, but it is unusual. I try to remain well away from analyzing any artwork for this young age. All sorts of whimsical drawings emerge at this time. I suspect fun here, from an advanced little boy. It's reinforced by the fact that the drawing is at the very top of the 9x12 paper, standing proudly on a pile of scribble with his bold name under it, not shown.

Figure 26

What to say about this little critter. After putting it on a light table, I could tell this little drawer wasn't content with the neck, which is itself unusual to find at this age. He didn't like the one leg (of four) nor the head treatment so he darkened or scribbled over them. He was using a marker, which is difficult to control.

Our next drawing in figure 27 shows an advanced stick figure girl. These don't normally come along until age 6 or 7. The little girl who drew this has either had some major adult or older child influence, or is quite ahead of her age group in many ways.

May I introduce you to the only stick figure in my collection of drawings by 4 year-olds....

Figure 27

I couldn't bear to put a box around her. She is the only thing drawn on a white page sized 9x12 inches. She is located in the upper left quadrant of the paper. This little artist has conformed in one way to her age, as the colors are subjective. Whatever looks good or is available at the time, works...black hair, green face, red body and a light orange ground line, also ahead of the crowd.

If this little stick figure doesn't make you smile you may have forgotten how.

Here are some more of the "not quite human, probably not really animal" sketches you will find in this general age group.

Figure 28

Figure 29

If none of these drawings represents your 4 or 5 year-old don't concern yourself, because the possibilities for this age group are endless.

Some things do start to develop such as stub arms from a definite body. Things from the side of the head with no body present might be ears as we adults identify them, but they also could be stub arms. They can also originate and spring from the area where the neck would be.

In this composite example you will also see how some children start to identify sex by hair and clothing.

Figure 30

The "unfinished" quality at this age and older is very common and does not bother the child in any way. While these drawings are balanced, in that they have two arms or legs, it is also routine to find them with only one.

Age Five

We continue with "anything goes." There may be attempts at structuring a picture but most kids do not want to tell a story with their drawing. There will be a vast variety of drawing ability. Don't frustrate yourself by trying to equate it to intelligence.

Floating items and bodies are very common until they end up grounded at the bottom of the page or by a plain line or a representation of grass.

Figure 31

Though the folks in figure 31 can strike us as primitive, this 5 year-old boy has developed a square body and a neck in the first figure. His second figure is a seated, profiled fellow and on a chair...good job! Stub arms and a head treatment on the first and no arms, no hair on the second. Two separate expressions on the same page.

The more common presentation is the goggle-eyed fellow here in figure 32 with his head set firmly on the body. Our little artist provides two very adequate "feet."

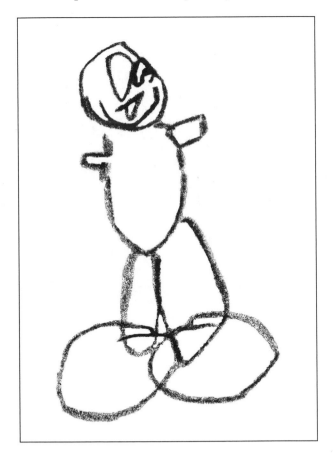

Figure 32

Speaking of feet, here is a very good pair attached to a floating female with stub arms drawn by a 5 year-old girl.

Figure 33

When I look at faces like this in figure 33, I begin to know what Piccaso meant when he said it took much of his life as a man to learn to draw like a child again.

In our next drawing, figure 34, you see what are often called "ray-arms" as they drop in a radial fashion in combination with the legs. This boy is $5^{1}/_{2}$. You saw ray-arms also on the crackerjack in figure 9.

You'll notice that the boy who drew figure 34 has enclosed the arms and legs. The hands are not true sun hands, but still a ray-like form. He has a huge grounding of green grass, a neck, and a large navel. We don't know what the vertical lines represent but quite often marks are used for balance. We'll revisit this figure in Chapter Five.

Figure 34

We can suspect that he has two representations of arms going on here. The aforementioned ray-limb combined with a "wing-arm." It is not uncommon to find wing-arms, such as in figure 35, all during these years and even older.

Figure 35

Figure 36

Figure 36 is the most well-defined drawing of arms as wings in my collection. There is a tendency to accept this and others almost as angel representations, but please, don't do that.

Analysts, in all honesty, have to confess that they do not know what the wing drawing represents. There are a few efforts to explain them. The only one that makes any sense to me is that the little folks who draw these may be rather emotionally needy. If you know the artist you will be able to see if he appears clingy or routinely needs an unusual amount of reinforcement or encouragement.

Figure 37

A 5½ year-old girl has completed a scene in figure 37, even though it floats. She has included a ground line and a sky line. The wheels at the feet are rare, but do show up now and then. We still have stub arms, the mandala sun, triangles in the roof of the house and lower bodies but she also tries to differentiate the two sexes.

She has combined the triangle-shaped roof and the rectangle to draw the house, which is common at this age, using two basic forms to build another.

The long blond hair is difficult to see and she does a feminine head treatment on what appears to be the girl.

Figure 38, is an example of arms extend horizontally, which you will see often from now on. When the body is drawn with a straight line it is a "Latin Cross."

Figure 38

Something else you see is "transparency." The stick arms and legs are later filled out with clothing. This is not a "stickman," as the body is round. Transparencies express an interest in what is under the clothing. This is natural with regard to those elements known to exist, even at an early age and whether or not there is sexual curiosity.

This 5 year-old girl may be representing her parents on either side of herself. Both blondes have feminine red mouths. The brown-haired man also has what appears to be a brown beard. I was advised sometime ago that children do not draw facial hair. Shall we reconsider that?

In figure 39 you see a true "Latin Cross" abstract.

Figure 39

Figure 40

You would be right to suspect a boy's countdown here, complete with the explosion...10-9-8-7-6-5-4-3 oops! 2-1-0... blastoff!

New forms now enter the scene, such as this rocket in figure 40. The drawing is done by a 5 year-old. He is storytelling with numbers and humans. He is a bit ahead of the game, as storytelling in a drawing most often begins in the sixth year. Some children never utilize it at all.

Rockets are, by their very nature, a phallic shape, but don't make the mistake of dwelling on this fact. Boys especially, draw a lot of guns (phallic) and airplanes (phallic) and submarines (phallic) and rifles (yup, phallic). I've known analysts and read analysts who seem to be scouring every drawing, looking for perversions. Please. These are the items that capture their young male imaginations, sometimes into adulthood. Much more on this in Chapter Five.

Figure 41

Most children are concentrating on the human form whether floating or grounded, an occasional rudimentary animal, a house, tree or flowers. The ground may be a simple line and the sky represented by sun or clouds.

Females are often portrayed with a triangular body which incorporates the dress, as in figure 41. Girls usually draw girls until adolescence, boys tend to draw boys.

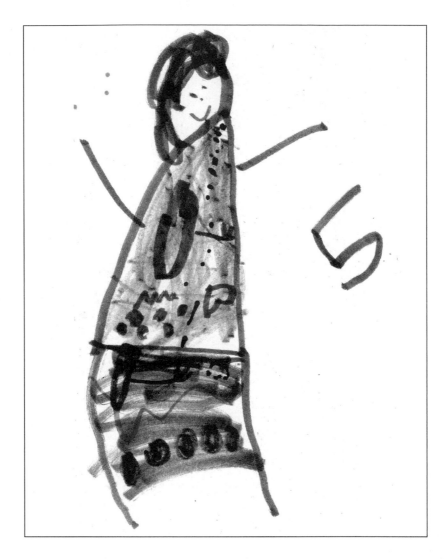

Figure 42

Here is another example of the triangle body. She has provided us her age. Notice all the design on the dress, considered feminine enhancement. The soft curved lines, circles and even an upside-down heart are a feminine representation. The arms going up here in figure 42 are not demonstrating excitement, but are meant as a balance to the overall form just as the stub arms are in figure 41.

Figure 43

And another by the same artist, as you can tell, by the similarity as well as her signature number 5. She puts herself in pants but keeps the triangle body. Though she started the blouse design with a checked pattern, she fills it in with circles. Remember, unless otherwise identified, the figure of the same sex drawn in the picture represents the artist herself.

Figure 44

This little lady in figure 44 is grounded at the bottom of the paper but gives the impression, by the flare of the triangle dress, that she's floated down on her parasol. Notice the flirtatious wink. We'll revisit her for a bit toward the end of Chapter Four.

The girl who drew the following female in figure 45 is the same age as the drawer of figure 44 but the presentation is totally different with the exception of the triangle body and triangular dress.

Figure 45 appears to be seated at the very bottom of the paper. She has no arms, perhaps because the drawer couldn't figure out how to add them to match the legs. Perspective and depth are usually not tackled until around age six.

Figure 45

Figure 46

Boys this age and older are inclined to use a square or box-like shape for the body of a male, at least some of the time when drawing the human.

Figure 46 shows such a fellow, floating still, but drawn well and the youngster has included a nicely scribbled ground line.

You've noticed a bit of chatter about the ground lines and we'll address all sides of this in Chapter Four. But for now, look back and try to see how it "feels" to you when you come across these ground lines.

Figure 47

Figure 47 shows more of the box-shaped body by boys. This is a representation of power and maleness, even though they may not be aware of it. It is rare to see strong shoulders represented on a female figure, but there are always exceptions. These might include a woman the child is a little fearful of, or an in-charge woman, such as a single mother who is responsible for the child's total welfare.

Notice the transparency of the head through the hat on the second figure—you know what the transparencies represent—those elements known to exist but hidden, often by clothing. But these see-through forms can exist in other shapes such as seeing through a person to the chair on which he is sitting, or a side view of a man in a boat with the bottom half of the man still visible through the boat.

Circles

The next drawing, in figure 48, shows us some new things. We have a larger group of humans, as well as a heavy concentration of circles.

Let's examine the very important circle figures of hands, feet, buttons and heads.

Figure 48

First, our artist has herself decked out in pants and nice bright colors and notice that her facial features are more fully drawn. This picture is about her.

Buttons are a sign of dependency, and what child this age is not dependent on others?

The circular hands and feet are a gentle representation of the extremities, carrying along the meaning of the circle in these obvious places.

The circle itself is drawn often by friendly, creative children. She surrounds herself with these circular "people" as a reinforcement to her social life. See the unattached head floating to her side on your right? The more, the merrier, and no body is necessary. (The head on the lower right is a teacher's smiley-faced approval.)

These little folks love to be the center of the action, and are content to be around others, even when they are not occupying center stage. Alone time may translate to downright lonesome!

The same charming child has sketched this next drawing, in figure 49.

Figure 49

Notice the treatment of the hands. I have never seen a better or more versatile example of sun hands opposed to her own "monster hands."

Her caption to the drawing is, "My mummy loves me (not seen well) when I am a little monster." (What a nice testimonial to her Mom, er, Mum.)

Look at the gentle circular sun hands on the mother. (Never mind the seven "fingers" in the form of rays. This is a balanced drawing in the mind of the child, and she may have even counted them.) The child realizes that the hands and feet must be represented differently on herself, because the figure is a "monster." What form does she choose? An aggressive one...feet with pointed toes and the attempt to draw fingers with points. Why? Because pointed fingers are considered threatening. But she is not an aggressive child, so she has to subconsciously settle for these almost pointed fingertips in this fun sketch.

Her claim to monster-hood is a tongue, sticking out in defiance, and a little pig nose. She chose pastels for Mum and a bright red devilish color for herself. Think Mum can handle her by one of those monster ears?

The next drawing is accompanied by a lengthy explanation which confirms what we are learning regarding circles and those who draw them in abundance.

Figure 50

This little visitor in figure 50 is described as a friendly creature from outer space who has come to play hide-and-seek all day and chess all night. You have noticed, of course, the extended use of circles in the drawing, and the creature has come to earth only to amuse and play with the artist. How fun to have the text inadvertently echo the meaning in the drawing.

Because our artist has described the eight eyes and two heads in words as well as her picture, she appears to not mind at all being at a disadvantage during games with her imagined playmate. The important thing is the company provided by her alien friend. Circles.

The circle form is drawn often by children who feel very close to their mothers. It is used also by children with creativity and new ideas.

The symbol of the circle stands for the beginning and the end, completeness and perfection, totality in and of itself. The circle is always considered a feminine symbol, as are all curved forms.

I have seen interpretations and various papers by therapists, expressing curiosity as to what the circle form means when drawn by abused children. It is often seen in these sad cases. It carries the identical meaning. Who would need the companionship of friends, the compassion of the mother and the creativity to cope, more than an abused child?

But don't let this image stick in your mind. The circle relates to the human condition, not in *any* way to abuse.

You have learned more than you realize to this point, and in the next chapter you'll be impressed by the new way you view a drawing.

Please review figure 8.

Chapter Three
From Six Through Adolescence

*"Every child is an artist. The problem is
how to remain an artist once he grows up."*
Pablo Piccaso

From this point onward we'll examine the stages of drawing, rather than trying to confine the progression to a specific year. We already know that we don't all proceed at a predictable pace, and the child may continue to draw in a favorite fashion for reasons of his own.

We'll start exploring the obvious and professionally recognized symbols sprinkled throughout, as the child's effort expands to routinely drawing scenes, rather than two or three objects on the page.

Age Six to Nine: The Visual Scene

The use of color now becomes more objective as the little artist picks up on colors in nature, as well as other items in his environment. There is also some subtle peer and adult "pressure" to color "correctly" or risk the consequences of teasing from the former and questions from the latter.

The house, tree, sun, humans and the more defined animal forms start to make an orderly appearance together consistently on the paper. The drawing may often tell a story or reflect things in his surroundings and imagination.

Certain objects are often not drawn in perspective. The human form can be larger than the house. One arm can be larger than the other to reflect an action such as waving. Objects are often drawn large and in a prominent way to reflect their importance to the artist.

The ground line will appear more often and more defined, as will the sky line. Ground and sky often do not meet in this stage, as there is difficulty showing perspective and space.

The human figure will generally be complete with the head, trunk, arms, legs, hands and feet. Some drawers will include the neck, ears and various adornments.

The drawings in this section will show you the various stages, but now we'll also start picking up information that is cataloged more directly in Chapter Five.

In the following drawing, figure 51, we see only four objects, the cloud, the house, the 6 year-old artist, and the ground line, but many bits of information.

Figure 51

Remember the reference to shading. It is always a form of anxiety. When the lower extremities are heavily shaded it can portray sexual anxiety (more on this later). He draws a ground line under himself, not the house. He is trying to settle and ground himself. He is large and out of proportion to the size of the house, wanting to emphasize himself or his needs.

The house has no door. The door is a well-accepted symbol of showing one's integration with others. The lack of the door means he is either a loner or lonely. He may have a situation related to the home that keeps him this way.

He has drawn large ears on himself. When a child has no hearing problem, this can reflect a concern that others may be talking about him. The large eyes also reflect a sensitivity or perhaps suspicion. There is no smile on the mouth but don't put a lot of stock in *any* smile. It can be normal for a child to draw a smiling mouth in spite of life's circumstances. The lack of hands shows some degree of helplessness, when considering the developed feet.

There is only one cloud but it hovers directly overhead, reflecting some sort of pressure on him. Fortunately it is not shaded and ominous.

This child could use a good friend in his life.

Figure 52

This first-grade boy is practicing forms of all kinds in figure 52, mostly animals. He ventures into a four-legged representation only on the lion at the lower left. How to draw forms with depth and make sets of legs look real will start to perplex a child after a year or two.

Children who want to draw and yet want to make the figure look real will compensate by drawing forms that don't require rigid dimensions. These may take the form of a human which can always be drawn from a frontal view, or animals and objects that don't require four legs. Note the following figures 53, 54, 55, 56.

Figure 53

Figure 54

Figure 55

Figure 56

Stick Figures

Figure 56 is a delightful representation of a stickman, which will usually start appearing now around age 6 or 7, if at all. You will find an occasional stick figure at age 5. This artist is almost 6.

There is no form that has created more curiosity and more analysis for yours truly than the meaning of the stick figure. Why? Simply because I have found so little written, let alone analyzed, regarding the stick form.

Some say the child picks up the form in school from adults or older children. I can agree with this. It happens often with many forms. Some say it is a form of egotism. Some say it is an expression of low self-esteem; others say evasiveness. Some show the example and say...nothing.

We can see why the stickman is attractive to draw. It is easy and straight to the point. Many adults have kept the form long after discovering it. But let's stay with the way the child uses it.

I am firmly convinced that the stick figure cannot be analyzed or well-defined *unless* the examiner knows the child—*and/or*—the circumstance of the drawing—*and/or*—the approximate stage of the drawer. Well now, is this an insurmountable task? Absolutely not. You should have the necessary information on any drawing you're considering.

Remember the 4 year-old who drew figure 27?

Figure 57

Let's take another look at her work compared to that of the 6 year-old boy on your right. It's generally accepted that girls develop, in certain ways, well ahead of boys. Her expression is "better" than his, but we cannot judge the intelligence of either. The stick form works for both of them.

That she may have learned and copied it from older folks only underscores her being a bit ahead of the pack.

Very young children who draw the stick figure when others are still drawing geometric forms with missing arms and legs may be considered, I feel, advanced. In what way? Artistically certainly, perhaps socially or emotionally, but let's call it a general readiness to learn and progress.

Should we say that this is egotism? The stick figure incorporates the head, trunk, arms, legs and sometimes the hands and feet, in a complete humanlike form. It provides an excellent format for those who know their human doesn't look realistic. Should the young child, under age 6, progress by drawing only himself in this way *and* continue to include others in less complete forms, it could relate to ego.

The artist who drew figure 56 still includes the gentle sun hands and feet, the trunk and arms form the Latin Cross, and he seems to be happily clicking his heels. The dog is not a stick figure. This boy will move on quickly to cartooning, I suspect.

Children who utilize the stick form, and not all do, will usually move through it quickly.

Figure 58

The little girl who drew figure 58 seems to be doing exactly that as she moves across the page. She is actually modestly clothing the female forms, with transparencies.

As the kids move out of the stickman form, the first to be embellished or drawn differently is the most important figure in the scene. In the following drawing, figure 59, it is easy to see how this can be interpreted as ego.

Figure 59

Her first-grade classmates and her teacher are drawn as minimal stick figures, though she did go back and give some of them faces and a suggestion of clothing. She may have run out of time, interest or both. The two rows of circles above the teacher are word balloons such as you would see in a cartoon, as she is reading to the class (but still indicate the artist's sociability).

Notice the position the drawing occupies on the page. This is a "movin' girl" located in the here and now and headed into the future. "Color me outta here."

The stick figure of herself is embellished nicely and

the legs even have a double line. What you cannot see however is the remainder of her very large name printed boldly clear across the page above the line. She has separated herself from her peers by all this, and also by the wavy line around the class and a large arrow pointing to herself. The tip of the arrow was partially erased along with her name when the teacher instructed the class to put names on the back of the paper.

So yes, in this case there is ego involved, and for as bright as she seems, couldn't it perhaps be justified?

In figure 60 below, the artist (in second grade) said that he is not in the picture. The stick forms in the submarine are so unimportant to the scene that one is left incomplete. This is the age when most start to abandon the form. He included them to show what is known to be inside a submarine—a transparency again.

Figure 60

The artist of the next drawing, about the same age, uses stickmen to show who is important and who is not.

Figure 61

The assignment in class for figure 61 was to say something nice about another student by drawing a picture and filling in the name of the person. Both names have been omitted.

The boy likes King Kong. The girl to whom the picture is dedicated is portrayed at the bottom apparently saying "The moveys (sic) are fun." She is not in stick figure form and her features, as well as her hair and hands and feet, are present.

The principals in the drawing, the ape and the fellow falling (we hope he's not the pilot), also have a body and extremities. They are important figures. The actress in the ape's hand is a stick figure, therefore not important. I felt the same myself, listening to Faye Wray scream all through the original movie.

Wait now, check the crowd of stick figure extras, and you'll see one important onlooker to the left of center. He has a body, hands and feet and is, without any doubt, the artist himself, enjoying the excitement.

This has nothing to do with ego in my opinion, but rather how important a person the stick figure is meant to portray in the drawing.

Just in the same way the younger child who had been using geometric forms for humans discovered and used stickman as an advancement, the older child abandons him. When the child, age 7, 8 and beyond starts drawing the more completed form of human *or not drawing the human at all*, poor ol' stickman diminishes in importance.

But don't weep for stickman. Great numbers of adolescents and adults pack him along and pull him out when they are forced to draw or diagram, saying they have no artistic talent.

In these adolescents and adults who utilize the stick figure, you will also find they may tend to use block printing rather than cursive writing in communications. The meaning is the same—don't get too nosey—I'll let you know what I want you to know—I'm a private person.

But now, let's get back to the other forms and the visual scene...

Here in figure 62 we see another story scene. This first grader has drawn a picture of herself and her friend walking in the park. You may think it appears to have been contaminated by a water spill, but her explanation is that it is getting ready to rain. Regardless of how this happened, we must agree it is very creative. After all, she does draw an abundance of circles.

The girls themselves are lined up like flowers though not attached in any way to the ground, and her minimalist drawings of buds, rather than flower heads may indicate that the attention should go to the figures. The hair is depicted almost like flower petals.

Notice the wing-like arms and she adds the same strokes on the legs for balance.

Figure 62

This first grader's colors are done in bright marker. If the skyline had been brought down any further the blue would have obscured the drawing. Even so, I doubt that she routinely connects the sky and ground.

Here is another example of the box-like shapes that boys draw for bodies at this age. The astronaut in figure 63 floats amid the stars and planets in a page totally filled.

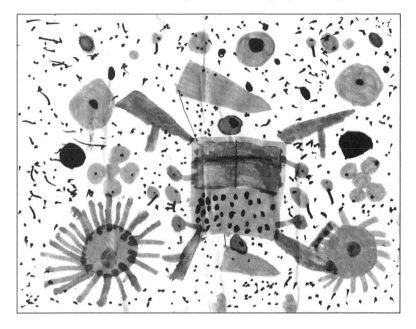

Figure 63

Figure 64

Figure 64 is a depiction of a world of children, all square bodied for this boy. Earth too, is a squared sphere.

In figure 65 our second grade boy has a little more on his mind, but still a strong, square body.

Figure 65

This little chap has fallen and fallen hard. Perhaps he takes the dog for a walk in order to see her? Even the tag on the dog's collar is heart-shaped. If he is this open regarding "love" at this age it will most likely continue through his life. Okay, his story is right out there, but, let's look around and see what he is saying without realizing it...

He's shown us the freckles on his nose, but what about the whites of his eyes which are colored a pale red? We know this boy has allergies, but he may just be stressing that he is wide eyed and star struck, considering the small pupils. The only other colors are a light colored green on the arms or shirt and blue on the legs or pants.

The drawing is done in pencil except for the hearts and the girl, who is drawn with a black marker, in order to make us pay attention.

It is unusual to see eyebrows at this age, a sign of vanity. The fact that he has eliminated ears on both himself and the dog indicates he may not be a good listener. Perhaps he's a day-dreamer? His button nose, as well as buttons on his body show his dependence.

We suspect the house is his own home because the doghouse is present, and he and the dog are a team. The house itself is solid, multi-dimensional, and has a chimney with loopy smoke curls. All of this suggesting that he feels secure there.

The proportioned door with a knob provides normal interaction with others, but the lack of windows and the smoke, which is a bit heavy, signal something further.

At least one window is considered normal for any drawing of a house. When missing, there is something the drawer does not want examined regarding either himself or the household. Too much smoke from the chimney reveals some tension in the house, or in himself. It may be a problem between siblings or between parents.

Perspective

Right around these two stages of drawing, the visual scene and storytelling, the child begins to make an effort to get perspective and angle correct in the drawing. No small task, and books have been dedicated in part to explaining exactly how some children accomplish the feat.

But not all do. Some children will give up drawing partly because of this issue around the age of nine or ten.

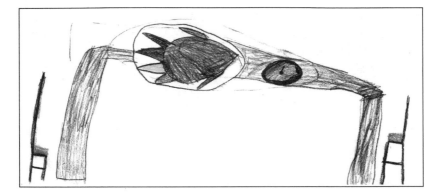

Figure 66

You can see the frustration in trying to show the turkey and the pie on the table by the erasures. Finally she settles for what is a "fold-over" and shows us two perspectives in order to complete her picture. The chairs present an additional problem, as do the table legs.

Figure 67

Here we see again, on the panda in figure 67, the same old challenge of trying to portray the correct aspect of animal legs.

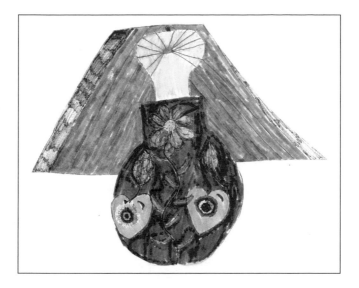

Figure 68

You would enjoy seeing this drawing of the lamp in color...aqua, yellow, fuchsia and a few tints in between, but let's look at the perspective. This nine year old girl will probably stay with drawing because she's quite good. In order to show us the "spokes" in the lampshade she does a transparency and a fold-over.

Figure 69

And this boy of the same age cannot quite manage the legs and seat on his chair doodle.

Figure 70

Figure 71 (Blow-up)

    Here's a cute depiction of a Halloween trick-or-treat costume—he went as "Grouch O'Marx"—in his explanation in the text. The welcome mat is on end so we can read it— another fold-over (and on Groucho's name, as well!).

Puff Pieces

Around age 9-10, you'll begin to see what I call "puff pieces." They show up in so many ways, as you can see by the composite in figure 72 and also by the word "panda" in figure 67 and in the shape of certain clouds. There is so little in the way of reference that I won't spend much time here, but this seems, to me, to tie into emerging hormones and the expansion of life in general. You'll find them in the drawings and doodles of both boys and girls.

Figure 72

Realism

Between the ages of approximately 9 to 12 children want their efforts on the page to look "real," and may start to convey emotion and relate to other people's feelings on the paper. They'll often show activity, travel and movement.

This is the point at which they'll become dissatisfied and give up on the "kid stuff" of art, if they can't seem to "get it right."

Dr. Betty Edwards tells us that at this point the individual—in order to draw easily and realistically—must switch from the left-brained, verbal identification of objects to the right-brained mode of allowing oneself to *see* without cluttering the view with language.

Do your children (and yourself?) a favor and expose them to her drawing instruction. Her books are referenced in the bibliography.

Figure 73

Wouldn't it be a shame if this girl did not continue to draw? Her church is sketched with all the elements in place. We can however, still see clues to the 11 year-old herself in figure 73.

The drawing tends to the left side of the paper. Mom is important, and the future (Dad is not around) seems a bit precarious. The little bush beneath the tree seems to be cautiously venturing down the step, into the future.

I know this child and she is a reader. Does the leaf style look unusual and creative to you? Like writing? When I mentioned this she said her art teacher had introduced the style. Kudos to her teacher. We'll cover more about trees in Chapter Six.

Figure 74

As realism takes over I notice the paper gets filled more often, perhaps just taking in all of life. Figure 74 is busy on its own, but this girl adds all the word balloons, apparently documenting an incident. Even the baby in the lower right window contributes "waa, mom, dad."

This tendency to add an explanation to the drawing means just what you might suspect—the drawer wants to be understood completely, whether on an emotional level or just for clarity. I've seen estimates that the number of children who add comments to drawings is about 18%. I tend to disregard statistics, but from my experience, this one could be close. Even back in figure 59, which could contain words in the word balloons, there are none.

Figure 75

Here again, in figure 75, the page is filled, the clouds are puffed, there is a glorious sun indicating parental love, plenty of eucalyptus for this koala bear to eat, and friends aplenty for this sociable girl in the form of flocking birds. The filled page demonstrates high energy and enthusiasm.

You see in figure 76 and figure 77 a sketching of real objects, which you will find children doing more and more.

Figure 76

Figure 77

Figure 78

This cut-away of a house by a 10 year-old is very full and busy. It is her house "after I am married," and detailed with happy things. There are no humans. The small stick figures you see in two of the rooms are dolls. All areas of the paper contain pastel colors and the colors appearing dark are blue, orange and light brown.

This house is a fine example of a common house transparency, or "x-ray" as a transparency is also called, to show what is inside and known to exist, the same as ears and head viewed through a hat or a stick form body seen through clothing.

Her good feelings about the house are reinforced by the wide walk or stairs to the doorway. The double doors with the large knobs show her openness to others, which is also echoed by the windows in the doors. A visitor can look in, and she can see out.

Figure 79

This drawing in figure 79 by a girl of the same age shows a cartoon of a nurse dog ready to treat the fleas that are pestering her patient on the right. She has started to give up on realism, at least some of the time, and go to a form that doesn't require an "apology." And do notice how cleverly she handles the problem of legs. She can do whatever she chooses to in a cartoon, and still feel accomplished.

Boys especially, will convert to cartooning or tracing to develop a picture or, depending on their interests, perhaps they'll choose space-oriented themes where they can have so much leeway.

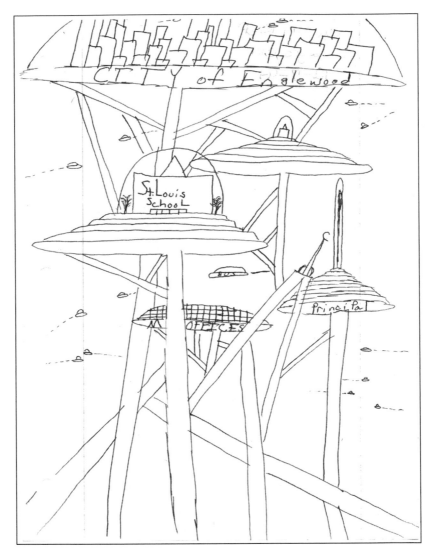

Figure 80

A 12 year-old boy with a science fiction form of his city and school, complete with futuristic transportation. He has drawing skill but doesn't choose to risk realism.

Adolescence

We can all recognize from those members of our own families and acquaintances just how many teenagers fail to continue to draw, in any form.

I have no statistics (would I trust them if I did?) but, judging by experience and observation, girls as a group are more likely to continue drawing than boys are.

I do notice though, that there seem to be far more male cartoonists than female, in both the political cartoon and comic strip credits.

With a little professional instruction an adolescent can develop the ability to demonstrate perception, light, shadow, scale and space. Then he or she can make the choice of whether the desire is present to continue in a chosen form, rather than simply drifting away from drawing by default.

The other choice will be abstract sketching in the form of design, which can become doodles for the rest of the adolescent period into adulthood, or abstracts in the form of fantasy or free-form design.

The youngster in figure 81 makes good use of the keyhole design. A great symbol, by the way, for the adolescent as he is trying so hard to unlock so many things.

Figure 81

Curves And Lines

A word regarding straight lines opposed to circular or curved shapes.

As you know the circular shape is considered feminine, and so is any other shape with a curve. The straight line, the box, triangle and any other form composed of rigid lines is considered masculine. But, guess what! Most of the time we will combine both forms in order to complete a drawing or a doodle.

Yet the drawing itself will have a definite bent toward either the masculine or the feminine, as you can see in the two doodles in figure 82 below.

Figure 82

As this is being written a gorgeous new building is taking shape at the University of Denver campus, the Newman Center for the Performing Arts. On each side of the entrance is a magnificent 24-foot stone bas relief panel of musicians, carved by three talented sculptors, two females and their male collaborator.

The reinforcement for me was delightful, when one of the women was quoted in The Denver Post..."he has the most generous heart, and does the best straight lines, while Kathi and I are better at curves."

Chapter Four
Colors, Numbers and Small Mysteries

"Art is an extension of language...an expression
of sensations too subtle for words."
<u>The Art Spirit</u>
Robert Henri

What is the main item a grandmother will have on hand for visiting kiddies? Yes, crayons of course, (a fresh box of 64 Crayolas® sets eyes aglow) along with plenty of paper and coloring pads. Almost all children take great pleasure in expressing themselves on paper even into their teens, and now you are learning how to read the messages.

Because this book deals with content doesn't mean we should not examine color in a brief way. As you read in the introduction, color is vital in healing therapy and carries important messages for the psychotherapist. These people deal with children and adults with serious conditions.

Gregg M. Furth, Ph.D., included in the reading list, is a leader in this field. He studied with Elizabeth Kübler-Ross (as has Dr. Bernie Siegel) as well as Susan R. Bach, the brilliant student of Carl Jung. He writes for the professional.

Mind-body connections, the conscious as well as the unconscious, are being explored and documented in detail these days. I have the greatest respect for those in the field.

But, our purpose here is to deal with the accepted significance related to the colors used in everyday drawings.

Colors

Choice of color is a subjective one. Often we avoid a shade or have an aversion to a color through an experience. I knew a man who could hardly look at a hot shade of pink, *only* because he was coloring with that shade as a child when he became violently ill with mumps.

You'll notice some children use every shade in the box and others select a few favorites. Some use whatever color happens to be handy.

Colors add to, but do not *tell* the story in a drawing. Pay attention to colors completely out of place, however.

RED

The color red represents energy and enthusiasm. It is associated with the blood of life, and with a warning or an emergency of any kind. A strong attention-getter, so pay attention if the child uses it in an unusual manner.

Particular attention should be paid to a red door on a house, but do remember that red doors are common in some neighborhoods, so investigate this. A house outlined in red needs to be discussed. A house colored completely in red should be referred to a professional.

Red is a popular shade used by most kids. The child who uses it abundantly demonstrates intensity, activity and possibly extroversion.

ORANGE

The color orange is accepted as a signal of self confidence and a general sense of joy and amiability. It can, conversely, represent a lack of discipline or a bit of hostility toward authority. Folks tend to be opinionated regarding orange–we like it or we don't.

YELLOW

The life-giving color of the sun. It symbolizes mental force, perception and curiosity. The child using a lot of yellow will respond to new ways of thinking.

Sometimes yellow, like sunshine, can be more appreciated in modest amounts. Designers tell us that a room painted bright yellow can bring on squabbling.

GREEN

Green represents the energy of nature, peace and renewal. It is considered a balancing color and a calming one. The color green is believed to still the physical and mental excesses and allow creativity and renewal.

BLUE

Blue is cool, it suggests distance and relaxation. It is the color of loyalty and inspires trust. A lighter shade of blue suggests nurturing and comfort.

The darker shades can be "engulfing" and relate to the consuming aspect of nature, such as the way the evening sky consumes the daylight or the way the ocean consumes the bright blue color the more deeply one plunges.

All shades of blue are thought to open the mind in order to share thoughts and ideas.

INDIGO

This lovely blue-lavender color is thought by many to represent the unconscious and intuitive side of our nature.

PURPLE/VIOLET

Associated routinely with royalty, spirituality and authority. Purple suggests superiority and the creative force. Those children who use a lot of purple in a drawing may demonstrate control and artistry, or may be in a period of personal growth. All shades of this color signal a universal appeal to imagination and excellence. Conversely, it can also reveal a self-absorbed person.

WHITE

The symbol of purity, cleanliness, and innocence. When a drawing reveals white on white paper it may indicate something concealed. Children find ways around this on white paper, such as outlining white clouds with a light blue, or drawing snow with a gray or silver crayon.

BROWN

Brown is the healthy color of fertility in nature. It symbolizes the earth and reproduction, as well as generosity. It can be interpreted in some cases as the need for emotional security, but is most often a confident color.

BLACK

The color black may be symbolized as the unknown. If used for heavy shading it has to be considered negative, so examine it carefully. It can project fear or a threat, but is also used as an attention-getter.

A picture containing a lot of black has to be analyzed thoughtfully, because it doesn't always portray gloom or depression, as many would have you believe.

Numbers

Whenever like objects are repeated in a drawing, take notice, and take a minute to count them. These will often relate to a significant number or year in the artist's life. It can be the current age or the age that a life trauma occurred or even such things as the number of members in the family.

A young woman drew a tree for me recently, in pencil. It was not the crown of a fruit tree yet she added four apple-like fruits when she was done. I casually asked her if anything of significance occurred to her at the age of 4. She acknowledged immediately that her parents were divorced when she was that age. These "coincidences" happen often.

Both Dr. Bernie Siegel and Dr. Gregg Furth report that seriously ill patients seem to know unconsciously in many cases, when their life will end. These expressions have shown up in children's drawings, and in adult drawings as well. Revealed objects, such as flowers or other objects in the sketch, will correspond to a unit of time related to their subsequent death.

This turtle in figure 83, walking up a path was drawn by a 7 year-old boy. It is one page in a story book but he manages to smuggle his age onto the turtle's back.

Figure 83

Figure 84

The boy who drew figure 84 had just turned 6 years old and had written this thank-you note. He has six tree trunks, though decided to include more tree crowns. The fourth tree trunk from the left is all connected, and there are six varmints and critters starting from the spider on the left of the trunks. Under the third trunk from the left are two critters of different colors. He is one busy boy.

Still on figure 84 you will notice the river at the right of the picture teeming with life, including one of those elusive "river octopus," complete with legs. You remember what a dilemma it can be for this age group to get a correct perspective? It won't bother him for a while yet.

Figure 85

And strangely enough, here in figure 85, the tortoise of an 11 year-old who was just bursting to turn 12 registers the same number of markings, 11 going on 12. Notice the conjoined line on two of the markings on the upper rear?

This drawing is from a story folder and on the other side is another picture, reproduced in figure 86. You'll notice the content bleeding through.

Figure 86

Eleven mountains in figure 86, same child. I make no pretense of trying to explain all this, it just is.

The most common things to find numbered in a drawing will be raindrops or flowers or the quantity of fruit placed on a tree. It may not reflect age, but the number of people in the family or anything of significance to the artist.

In the following pages we'll see some fun sketches and one tragically sad one.

Figure 87

This 9 year-old girl has decorated her tree with nine very prominent "oranges." The other small dots are meant to be budding fruit and many green leaves.

In the next drawing, figure 88, you see the 5 year-old has included the proper number of raindrops. Though you cannot see it she includes a fifth line on the west of the house, that is almost the same color as the paper. These lines are an encapsulation and meant to protect the house from any rain. We'll deal with encapsulation shortly.

Figure 88

Figure 89

Above, in figure 89, is a scribble with six abstract forms floating overhead drawn by a 6 year-old. It is not unusual to find scribbling and abstracts at any age.

On April 20, 1999 here in Colorado, as most Americans know, a teacher and twelve students lost their lives in the Columbine High School tragedy.

Rachel Joy Scott, a lovely 17 year-old, was one of the thirteen slain. She drew this picture, often referred to as *Rachel's Tears* or *Thirteen Tears,* in her journal during class the morning of the shooting.

Her family believes that Rachel knew the end of her life was near because of certain entries in her journal, and they, among many others, consider her picture a prophetic one.

I sincerely appreciate both the time spent talking with me and their permission to use the drawing. The family invites all to visit their web site, www.racheljoyscott.com for complete information.

The rose has appeared in some of Rachel's other drawings, always with the thin, thread-like line surrounding it and often including the dark drops, resembling blood, emerging from the thread. She drew the rose, as she had in other drawings, without thorns, which are thought to represent sin and pain. The rose itself is a representation of perfection, as well as life's mystery. Her journal and her life indicate that Rachel Scott was a devout Christian.

The symbolism in the drawing is stunning. Feminine eyes (the way we see the world) shedding thirteen clear tears (the victims) on the unfolding rose (purity, perfection, earthly love and rebirth, therefore, the Godhead, with three leaves representing the trinity) all encompassed by a fragile thread (lifeline) containing eighteen drops of blood (life). She died in her eighteenth year.

The drawing originates in the intellectual sphere, showing the tears meeting the rose in the emotional present. The rose is based in the instinctual sphere, leaving room to the right, the future—for the unknown—for faith.

Rachel's Tears

Figure 90

Here we are in the section christened *small mysteries*. The more you know or can confirm about the child who has drawn the picture you are examining, the more sense your explorations will make. The drawings we see expose things about the child's thinking or situation, and in some cases, their mood at the time.

I remind you again, this is not the reading of tea leaves or the casting of chicken bones. No psychic ability is involved, only a responsible interpretation of years of work by dedicated professionals.

Encapsulation

When the artist encloses herself or anything in the picture, especially in an unusual way, you have a child trying to protect herself. Period. From everything or from a specific person or situation if she has any kind of border around herself. Protection from someone if she has the other person encapsulated, or from something if she has an object enclosed with any sort of border.

It can often be as simple as the enclosure of the house in figure 88. Because there is a very large door with a knob, and because she herself, is not in the picture, it seems she is indicating those large raindrops are meant exclusively for the large flowers.

Some troubled children will encapsulate each member of the family in a drawing. What a sad situation, trying to isolate each member from the other.

In figure 91 this 5 year-old boy is trying to protect himself from something. Perhaps bad dreams? The closet monster? We cannot speculate further without facts.

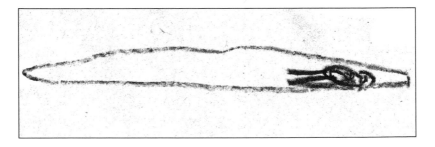

Figure 91

Figure 92

The situation is sadly similar with this helpless boy, missing arms and hands, in figure 92.

Put your pressure skills to work on the line around him to see how he drew it. The rounded line at the bottom shows the starting and stopping pressure from left to right, then up from the lower right, across the top and down to the lower left. Now check how he made the body and feet.

The next figure, 93, drawn by a 6 year-old girl, is another form of encapsulation but done entirely by crayon. Do you see the elaborate dark (blue) crosshatching holding her in place? The clouds and rays of the sun are also imprisoned, keeping everything away from her.

She has no feet, no ground line, no stability, and this can also indicate depression or insecurity. We don't know her situation. She draws herself without ears. Could she have a hearing problem? That fact could account for the discomfort in the drawing. More likely, she is simply choosing not to relate to something at home or at school. There is a cloud directly over her and her ponytail points to the other one. Pressure or problems.

Figure 93

Her feminine features are stressed by the attention to the mouth and eyelashes. Those lavender eyes are large, and here again she may be suspicious and sensitive.

Take a minute to see how the next drawing in figure 94 makes you feel. The 6 year-old has herself encapsulated and sadness is rampant throughout this entire pencil sketch. The world seems to be raining on only her and erasures indicate she's looking for her place in it.

She too, stresses her femininity—eyes, mouth, waist and a necklace. Her pupils are small, indicating some self-absorption, or do we see a hint of hostility, echoed by the

Figure 94

strong shoulder line and squared footing? While we don't quite understand what the encapsulation is in the drawing, we know what it represents.

Pay attention to the large head which is not unusual for children to draw, but starts to diminish in size from this age on. When it is accented in this fashion by the hair (heavily shaded) and size, it indicates self-esteem. She also accents the sturdy neck, which indicates a total acceptance of the body. She likes and thinks highly of herself and her abilities. The eyebrows are very heavily drawn and close to the eyes, and while this can mean that the person is uninhibited, in reality she does have prominent eyebrows.

What do we know about her personally that might account for all this need for protection? To begin with, she's a precocious 6 going on 7 and has two teenage sisters. With two teenage girls running rampant most of us might feel the same need, regardless of our age.

The family had moved to the U.S. recently, forcing her to leave behind school, friends and family. Her parents had been separated, and only reconciled shortly before the move. If she had a bad experience with school or a friend on the day she drew this, we can totally understand.

Again, try not to jump to conclusions, no matter how ominous the sketch may appear.

Trajectory

Analysts will tell you to always check the trajectory of movement in a drawing. What would happen in the next frame if it were a movie? This is most obvious in requested family drawings to work out aggression, for instance. If that baseball swing is completed who does it hit? If the car keeps moving will it run over someone?

The 6 year-old on the skateboard in figure 95 is happily heading for a bright blue puddle as he's being pulled by his eyeglass wearing (?) dog. His own eyes seem to reflect lightning in his glasses. I'd be very surprised to learn that this boy does not wear glasses in reality. This is an assigned drawing of rain in class, yet he's still having a good time. Big splash coming up.

He draws the square body of preference for this age on both of them, and has buttons showing his dependency.

Figure 95

Figure 96

The artist of figure 96, a second grade boy, shows the exact trajectory of his war scene. Notice he is protected in his "war box" encapsulation. He has a powerful square body but the figures who are "catching it" are mere stick figures. He appears to be transmitting to use his weapons and is one step away from the fighting, even giving himself a light bulb with which to conduct his war.

Body Image

It is always good if you know the child who is drawing himself or herself in the picture. Many impressions can be given by self portraits, some flattering, some not so, but it will give you many clues how the child sees himself. We'll see serious examples in a later chapter.

The 6 year-old who drew figure 97 also drew figure 98 at the same time, titled of course by the teacher.

Figure 97

Figure 98

It is worth noting that the boy actually is pigeon-toed, as he shows in figure 98. He has erased, trying to portray himself correctly. Notice the crown he had placed on his head and then erased. He has a healthy self-esteem and is the youngest in the family, so may well think of himself as "the little prince." And that's okay, isn't it?

Do you find figure 99 uncomfortable? A little sad?

Figure 99

This drawing came to me in a group of pictures that the teacher knew nothing about, other than the age and grade. The boy who drew it is 5¹/₂. He draws a black house with no door, a dark cloud overhead, but the boy himself is of great interest. I wish we knew about him.

The coat is red, the nose and mouth are red and "smeary." Of real curiosity is the black line down the middle of the chest. The arms are almost in a crucifixion pose. This child may have asthma or an equally serious problem. The ears are large (earache or people talking about him?) and the eyes are alerted and suspicious.

He is as tall as the house and the tree, therefore feels he should have attention paid to him.

The 9 year-old girl who presents us with figure 100 creates a modest presentation of a trim curly haired girl with a studious look. Squares, such as she draws for glasses show a desire for organization and structure and buttons show her dependence. Her hands are tucked behind her in an expression of indecision and a tendency to avoid conflicts or evade a situation. Her small feet are shaded to add stability. But wait, let's look at...

Figure 100

...the way the form is positioned on the page. This changes things. The girl herself is bright and pretty but not as portrayed here. She is chubby, with a straight bob and round glasses which diminish her lovely blue eyes.

In Chapter One we discussed this placement of a figure on the bottom of the wide axis (figures 11 and 12). This particular girl is neither conceited nor domineering. She is that rare exception, the child who retreats into fantasy as a coping mechanism at times in her life. She spends much of her private time with television, movies and books, rather than other children. There is a tendency to dwell on past incidents and some depression. A figure placed low and isolated at this age identifies an emotional problem.

Figure 101

In figure 102 a 6 year-old boy has drawn what he says is himself. The body was scribbled in pencil, then completely covered with red marker. His eyes appear to be looking down at his body. He eliminates the mouth, which

Figure 102

some analysts say indicates depression, guilt and a rejection of affection. Though there is bright yellow sunlight in the upper left, he surrounds himself with blue raindrops and stands in a blue rain puddle. The extremities and his head treatment are drawn in heavy black marker. I would question what he does not like about his body. With the missing mouth and bright red body might he be obese?

Vamps And Vixens

Oh, these little girls are a hoot! They celebrate their femininity and give their dads fits in later years. This category is my own, so far as I know. (I have seen a "seductress" referenced in abuse, which is totally different.)

The vixen drawings are hip, modern and almost always have two girls present in the sketch, sometime with boys as—well—props. The artist usually overshadows the other girl in some way.

These are the girls who are interested in and curious about the opposite sex from an early age (not that they act on it) and are very social. When cliques of "ins" develop socially, they are among them.

Figure 103

Our vamp in figure 103 is 6 years-old, poor dad. She has given herself a rather, ah, developed set of mammary glands and put large red lips on both figures. Her friend in figure 103 is probably female considering the hair and lips but appears to be no great, um, competition. She grounds herself with shaded shoes while her friend floats, footless.

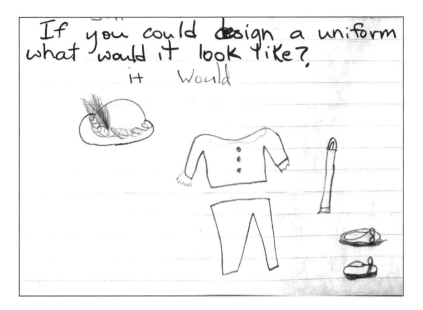

Figure 104

The drawer of figure 104 leaves no doubt what a 10 year-old vamp uniform should look like in response to her teacher's question. Flirtatious loops (seeking excitement) and a feather on the hat (a desire for attention) and bows on the shoes indicate she likes flattery. Rest assured those pants are leotards, the midriff top speaks for itself, and a lipstick tube is a most sensual symbol. Consider the action of the tube itself and the shape of the lipstick.

In Chapter Two, figure 44, is that little vamp with a parasol that I promised at the time we would revisit.

She floats there in full makeup. A big red mouth, long eyelashes complete with a wink, and fully developed nose. Remember, this little girl is only a 5 year-old.

Pockets on a dress at hip level are considered to be very feminine. She has added bows to them which, as you've just learned, show a desire for flattery.

All in all, with the explicitness of today's advertising and programming, as well as the openness of families and acquaintances, it's difficult to keep a child in an innocent environment. We're not in Kansas anymore, Toto.

Figure 105

The vixen on the right in figure 105 has sketched herself and her "cool" friend. Her eyes are larger, lashes are longer and the breast area better defined. They both sport voluptuous lips. The names are blocked out, but she had both her first and last name in two separate places and her friend's first name only. Age? Second grade.

Their skin is done in bright yellow as are the small convoluted arms. The lack of arms and hands betrays her childishness and some sense of helplessness. All noses are symbols of power striving and sometimes sexuality. No noses. Missing noses reveal a lack of love or nurturing, or limited vitality. Being a vamp, she'll, sadly, be searching quite eagerly for love and acceptance when dating begins.

Figure 106 is amazingly well constructed for a—brace yourself—5$1/2$ year-old girl! Mind you, others her age are drawing circles and boxes for bodies. Stylized bodies, stylish clothing, complete with a poodle sweater, huge red lips on herself and look at the noses. Watch out.

Figure 106

Figure 107

Figure 107 was done by the 9 year-old girl on the left who portrays herself as dancing (spelling isn't her long suit). She leaves no doubt how she feels about her older sister, and even includes some jabbing pencil marks on her face which she acknowledges, in fun, as pimples. She portrays her sister with one rather aggressive hand, which she may have to dodge occasionally.

Mom is feminine with lips, eyelashes and curls. She likes Mom, as she is placed on a little pedestal to be as tall as Dad. The position of his hand on Mom's abdomen may have just evolved in the drawing, but even so, indicates a comfort level with the playfulness that she may have witnessed. Notice the mother's arm carefully drawn behind his, in order not to interfere with the positioning.

Dad is okay in her eyes, gentle hands, possibly a tease not unlike herself, and she views her touching parents as a close team.

We have here a young vamp, extremely interested in flirting and the interplay between the sexes.

Chapter Five
Some Basic Symbols

"It is interesting to observe that children from many and distant lands will draw the sun in exactly the same way, as though they had gotten together and agreed upon it."
Joseph H. DiLeo, M.D.

We have touched on many of these symbols to this point. Now, with that exposure, it becomes easier to define and explore the integration of the symbol into the drawing.

Trees are of such importance and variety that we'll devote an entire chapter to them.

You must give yourself, and the artist of the drawing, as well as the symbol itself and the way it is used, a degree of latitude in your interpretation. Too often, I find that rigid definitions can distort the actual meaning in a child's sketch. Why otherwise, are there so many different opinions among analysts? Consider the nuances and interactions in any drawing. Always lean to the side of generosity if there is any question regarding the use of a symbol. Common sense must reign, coupled with knowledge regarding the artist of the drawing.

Every effort is made to present practical opinions and sensible definitions in these pages.

The Sun

One of the most prominent and universal symbols to appear in the drawings of children is the sun. Almost all renditions I have seen of the sun in children's drawings contain rays indicating warmth and luminosity. (I beg you please, to send me a copy if you have a genuine drawing that does not. I have only one.)

Why is this so? Because the sun represents parental love. Or, in rare cases, the need for it.

Analysts in the past have tried to tie the sun to the love of the father, and mother love to the moon. When it became more and more obvious that the sun was present in many drawings and the moon in only scant offerings, and often there was no father figure involved in the child's life, it became practical to rethink all of this. It is not uncommon to find any type of discipline in a state of flux, most certainly psychology.

Some analysts have offered that the sun represented the father when placed on the left side and the mother when drawn on the right. Some said the opposite positions ruled. Some said that it was often included in the drawings of young children and had no significant meaning. (!?)

It has been sensibly accepted by many to simply mean parental love.

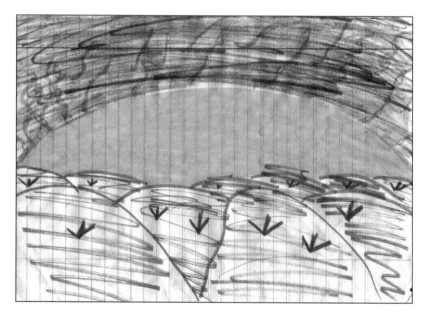

Figure 108

Otherwise, how to explain this overwhelming full-page expression in figure 108? I know this 9 year-old girl. She has almost full time attention from her mother at home and feels abundant love from both parents. Without these facts, I would interpret the drawing the same way.

When the sun is incorporated into drawings of older teens and adults it can mean a need for, or a lack of, personal warmth in their lives. Unless you learn otherwise, the need reflects a parental figure.

Children who tend to anthropomorphize (give human attributes or features) in their drawings will often choose to use the sun, as this child does in figure 109.

My sense is that the sun is viewed as an omniscient and comfortable presence, much like the typical parent, at least to the preteen child.

Figure 109

While the sun as a common symbol, is often included in drawings of youngsters, We should certainly not read anything into drawings made without the sun. So little time, so much to draw.

There is however, one interpretation I've seen from more than one source regarding balloons and the sun, that should be considered. The theory that balloons floating toward the sun indicate the child's desire to spend more time with, and receive more affection from, the *father* (or we could read *parent*). This could apply to many children and fathers, certainly, in this day and age.

The balloons are floating in figure 110, toward the sun but are still attached to the child. Does the meaning change? In order to analyze these representations you must know the artists and their circumstances. Keep all interpretations in the back of your mind, but also consider the nuances.

Figure 110

Figure 111

Here, in figure 111, the balloons are floating free without doubt, but there is no sun in the sky. Does that change the meaning? Yes. It can mean a desire to rise above a situation in the artist's family life or environment.

This is basically an expression of lightheartedness and freedom, done in blues and greens, with a happy red smile on the anthropomorphic face of the center balloon.

Notice the ground lines on both of these drawings. They are full and rounded, rather hilly, as if to give their balloons a staging place in order to float, free of obstacles. Which brings us naturally to......

Ground Lines

You've noticed comments regarding ground lines as we've gone along and we need to draw some distinctions. Those in the previous two drawings are used well for a seemingly definite purpose, which is to accommodate the intention of the picture. Ground lines in other drawings throughout the book serve a similar purpose.

To paraphrase myself, "sometimes a ground line is just a ground line."

When a child begins to draw scenes rather than just an object or two, he will locate the picture at the bottom of the page and use that as an implied ground line. Or he will draw in a line of ground or grass. This is a representation of a normal scene or realism.

Remember this little guy from figure 34 with his ray hands? There are other things that I now want you to look at in figure 112.

Figure 112 (34)

The drawing itself has a lost, insecure feeling to it. When a huge navel is drawn it represents being lost in the world, and some say a desire to return to the womb. The head is completely detached from the neck and body. He compensates by including a great expanse of ground underfoot to support himself, to give himself a secure base.

If you will turn back to figure 99, the boy drew what almost appears to be a dangerous ground line. He actually floats above it. This further reinforces the interpretation of the drawing.

Back again to figure 51, the child has a ground line drawn only under himself, as I mentioned, in his search for stability.

So always look carefully at the ground line in the picture. If it is exaggerated for a purpose, such as growing large flowers, then you know it all meshes, and does not necessarily mean a search for stability.

Figure 113, below, is done by a 10 year-old boy with aspirations of becoming a football player. It was drawn in pencil, then colored with pastel greens and blues.

Figure 113

Notice first the minor encapsulation, done by the colored sky and ground. The clouds are stormy and appear to be raining on him. One is directly overhead. He has on a helmet and a smile, but the teeth are quite aggressive, perhaps meant to convey how tough he is, or wants to be.

He draws a deep ground line but he stands in a low spot, and is sadly without feet. Though the drawing can almost be seen as a happy one, he is in a funk.

What do we know about him? An intelligent child, he is one of a large family, whose parents are working long hours. He is sedentary and overweight. His unhappiness and insecurity are showing without his knowing it.

Pay attention to all ground lines and see if there is anything different about them. Ask yourself if they fit within the idea of the drawing or if they are added for no apparent reason.

A line drawn across the bottom of a page always represents the need for added stability.

Skylines

Children of all ages will draw a picture without trying to illustrate the sky in any way. I don't attach any kind of significance to this. They will usually include clouds or a sun or a treetop, as a way of using the top of the page (remember figure 8) when they are old enough.

It is however, somewhat unusual to find a drawing illustrating a large background of sky, without a ground line such as in figure 114. All of this colored sky is not an encapsulation though, as shown in figure 92.

The second grade girl who drew figure 114 had a difficult time as she tried to place herself on the horse, She finally gave up in frustration, as seen by the erasure. All sky and no ground line reflect her insecurity.

In figure 115, our 6 year-old shows himself beside a silver colored sun whimsically sketched as a house. He uses the circular clouds drawn in metallic gold, as a ground line. To his right is a radiant cloud bleeding through from the back of the drawing. Is his home heaven on earth for this little guy?

He draws in the emotional sphere toward the bottom of the page which is normal for his age. He shows no desire

Figure 114

Figure 115

to progress any further to the right, to the future. His decorated hat shows that this charmer is happy at center stage, and also by this positioning, not an aggressive child.

He has no reason to add a sky, even if he were so inclined, because the entire drawing is already "sky."

The skyline drawn in figure 116 is the kind we must check carefully against the rest of the picture.

Figure 116

The artist is a first grade girl. She stands on a very sharp, aggressive ground line, which you'll notice is modified beneath her, compared to that under the table. There is an ominous cloud directly overhead. The skyline is actually a pleasant blue, as is the cloud, but the cloud is cross-hatched with a dark gray scribble.

Glancing at this picture, with no knowledge of it, one could be puzzled by the form at the lower left, and also what might be construed as a baby on the table (done by the way, as a fold-over). But we have a small amount of information.

The picture came to me from a friend in a seasonal group of Thanksgiving drawings. That "baby" is a turkey on the platter and it's anthropomorphized with human facial features. The form at the left is probably meant to be a canoe. I say this because other drawings in the group had canoes included in various Pilgrim/Indian drawings.

This might confound and disappoint some analysts I've known who love to look for phallic symbolism. Should they choose to stay with an interpretation of that type, they'd be forced to now consider it a female symbol. All boats and water are feminine symbols, as are bottles, cups, glasses and other types of containers. But more on this later, now back to the skyline.

This type of a dark and narrow sky, especially with the ominous cloud directly over her, indicates she feels some sort of pressure. Interpret all narrow lines at the top of the page as something hanging over the artist.

The fact that she draws herself so small compared to the table, without hands and feet which are usually present by first grade, and standing on such a ground line indicates her sense of helplessness. But there is usually an easy explanation. What if she is a "vegetarian" and has to endure a large turkey dinner with family and friends? My own granddaughter took this vegan position at age five.

It could be this simple. It could explain the face on the turkey, and all of the other stresses.

When children reach the point where they connect the sky to the ground, and not all do, it seems to carry the same general meaning as a page that is completely filled with drawing. As you may remember, that means a high energy level and an enthusiasm for life.

The House

A drawing of a house will often provide you with a great deal of information. Some analysts have said the house can represent a parent, usually the mother, or even symbolize the individual himself. I can't seem to wrap my mind around that. The more common interpretation is that the house symbolizes the artist's attitude toward the home and the relationships in the home, therefore, issues of security and nurturing.

The color chosen is only important if the house is red or in some cases, black. Outlined in red, the child's home situation should be examined. Any house completely colored in red, should have a professional consultation. When the drawing of the house is outlined in black, unless the entire sketch is done in black for some reason, look to any other indicators of pressure or unhappiness on the page.

In addition, what you want to examine in the sketch of the house is the overall presentation. The normal drawing of a house contains certain elements, namely a roof, often a chimney, walls on all sides, a window or windows, a door and some sort of base or ground line.

Figure 117

Figure 117 reflects these elements and even a couple of others, with one major exception. This 9 year-old girl uses the bottom of the page for the base of the house. We like to see the house with a base of its own, because otherwise it reflects an insecurity relating to situations in the home. We'll return to this pleasant little house in due time to examine other aspects.

On the other extreme is the wobbly presentation done below in figure 118. The 6 year-old boy who drew this is not a good student. Notice that it is not grounded by even the paper's edge. The walls are weak, no window is present, and the roof and the side wall are crosshatched. He stresses the doorway and what seems to be a covered window but there is no doorknob for entry.

Figure 118

The house is placed at the right side of the paper and the boy is described as quite aggressive. Walls relate to the strength of the ego. Because his walls are of light pressure and even the color is light, we can assume he is vulnerable and bluffs a lot. Crosshatching, such as we see in the roof and wall, is described shortly.

Let's interpret some individual meanings of the parts of the house.

Roof

The roof represents the fantasy area of life, which is the ability to daydream and to imagine. The size of the roof is important, rather than the shape.

- A shallow roof or a line for the roof shows the artist may lack the ability to daydream. This could affect, for instance, the capacity to enjoy a bedtime story without visual stimulation.
- An overly large roof, or an extremely detailed one, indicates an over-involvement in fantasy, and the child may be withdrawn or reluctant to have routine contact with others.
- Drawing an emphasized or reinforced roofline, to include one with heavy pressure on the outline, indicates a defense against the possibility of fantasy taking control.
- A heavily shaded roof indicates the drawer may be anxious about her ideas or way of thinking.

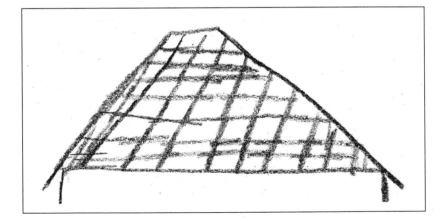

Figure 119

- Crosshatching, such as we see in figure 119 has more than one explanation. Some say it suggests a strong conscience and a sense of guilt to go with it. Some say one is trying to forget something about the house or a person in it. Others say the child is busily trying to put the facets of his life together.

  One reminder, don't overlook the fact that the child may simply be trying to realistically portray shingles on the roof.

  Try to sort this all out according to indicators in the drawing and what you know about the child.

Figure 120

Here in figure 120, is an example of a busy, detailed roofline. This is from a drawing bursting at the seams with "stuff," however, so we must consider the entire picture (remember the high energy level of those who draw a filled picture). She does incorporate just about everything possible on the roof though, including a dated television antenna. Her ability to fantasize and enjoy daydreaming is just as broad and wide as this snippet of her picture.

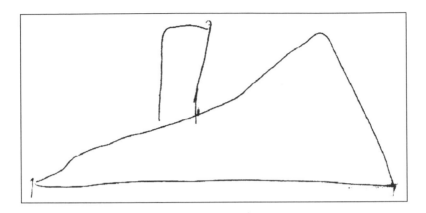

Figure 121

Chimneys and Smoke

A natural extension of the roof is the chimney. Many analysts claim the house is incomplete without one. Some put great stock in a missing chimney, saying there is no escape for the heat in the house, or expression of warmth inside the house, without one.

Personally, I reserve judgement regarding missing chimneys, and here is *one* reason. In *Analyzing Children's Art*, Rhoda Kellogg documented 3,277 house drawings of children age five to eight, in order to find the frequency of chimney designs. 1,520, had *no* chimney. It appears normal for some children to simply not include a chimney.

If the chimney is included it can, most certainly, be interpreted.

Some young children have trouble getting it placed on the roof, and the right-angled chimney is common. The little girl who drew figure 121 took care of it nicely by flattening the angle of the roof rather than cocking the chimney. Figure 120 also has the chimney placed on the flat surface of the rooftop.

- A missing chimney can indicate passivity in a child, *or,* some say, a lack of psychological warmth in the home.
- An extremely large chimney or a reinforced one can represent concern about the warmth in the home, either too much or too little. It can show concern about power. By the age of eight and beyond it may show concern by the artist about his own masculinity.

- A chimney can be can be a phallic symbol. The design will leave little doubt, if the child is demonstrating in this way. It's found more often in the drawings of older boys. If the chimney, drawn by a male, is toppling or has the upper section missing, the meaning is a feeling of inadequacy.
- A noticeably elongated chimney, drawn by a male indicates a striving for virility.

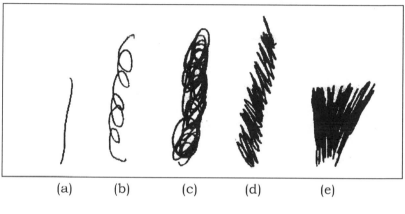

(a)   (b)   (c)   (d)   (e)

Figure 122

In order to easily understand smoke you have only to draw cach of these and see how you feel as the pen or pencil moves.

- (a) A little wisp that demands no energy. This is a token drawing of smoke. Some analysts say this is an indication of little warmth in the home.
- (b) Loopy curls. Generally this type of smoke gets the best response from the analyst, indicating a pleasant warmth in the house.
- (c) Heavier looping covering itself. A measure of tension is building in the artist, concerning the house or someone who lives there.
- (d) Heavy jagged angles. Anger relating to an aspect of the house or an occupant.
- (e) A thick dark plume. Explosive feelings, or extreme resentment of something present or someone who lives in the house.

We have not yet discussed "handedness," which is whether one uses predominantly the right hand or left hand. In graphology we do not try to determine this in most cases because it doesn't matter. The analyst can be easily fooled. The lefties compensate in marvelous ways.

In drawing however, it is accepted that it is easier and more natural for the left-handed artist to draw a profile facing right, and for the right-handed person to draw any profile facing left. This is not to say it is always done so.

My reason for bringing this up is to guide your thinking regarding the direction the smoke may take. Some analysts say this can indicate parental pressure when it veers sharply. This can be true, but only if we figure the pressure points correctly. The pressure always comes from the opposite direction the smoke is headed. Therefore, smoke veering sharply to the right, as though blown by the wind, would indicate pressure from the mother or other female relatives, perhaps.

Smoke drifting lazily to the right *could* show more interest at the moment in the father, or to the left a tendency to be with the mother.

But here is the clinker. If the child is a lefty the tendency will be to pull the smoke left, and you *may* notice the looping will be counter clockwise. If right-handed, the smoke will tend to curl naturally to the right and *may* be drawn clockwise.

Walls

The walls of the house relate to ego strength. You and I, in analyzing them, have to be totally aware of how the child (or any age person) might unknowingly try to manipulate this symbol. In other words, we have to be smarter than the wall. (!) Let me give you the commonly accepted interpretations, then we'll chat.

- Walls drawn in faint lines show a lack of ego strength.
- Thinly drawn walls indicate weakness or a vulnerability.
- Strong walls suggest a strong ego, and confidence in the self.
- Crumbling walls indicate a deteriorating or dis-integrating personality.
- Unusually tall vertical walls indicate the personality has an active fantasy life.

- Overemphasized horizontal walls indicate a practical nature and the need to be grounded.
- Emphasis on walls, by retouching, shows a need to add or to maintain ego strength.

Figure 123

Figure 123 is a composite of the vertical dimension as opposed to the horizontal dimension of a house. I see many tall, wildly proportioned houses, some of which are included in these pages. Knowing that most children have some degree of fantasy life, I see no conflict with this definition, nor that of the horizontal house, even when it is not exaggerated.

We always want to consider the intent if we see a crumbling wall. Some children like the look of brick peeking through stucco, or are storytelling with a wall. Children who have been through serious earthquakes will draw cracked, crumbling walls for years after.

Notice the reinforced walls on the house on your left. This is an example of trying to strengthen the ego, even as the heavy baseline is a grounding maneuver.

When you know something about the artist you have good clues to decipher any weak or wobbly walls. Do not forget to incorporate the page diagram (figure 8) into the wall interpretations, as we did in figure 118. A weak wall on only the right side, for instance, should lead you to question the artist's feelings about the future.

When you spot a really sturdy wall ask yourself if it is truly strong or merely reinforced. We'll see more examples of walls in completed drawings in Chapter Nine.

Windows

We touched on houses drawn without windows in figure 65. The child who eliminates windows does not want anyone prowling around in his thoughts and feelings. And as you remember, it can also mean there is something problematical about his home situation. A blocked or colored-in window (such as you see in the doghouse in figure 65) carries the same meaning.

- If all windows appear above the first floor in the house it indicates the artist does not want people to see inside.
- Closed shutters are a barrier against interaction with others.
- A window, especially a small, colored-in window on the door (or the house, mentioned above) is also a barrier to any interaction. An "X" type windowpane reinforces this interpretation.
- A small window is an indication of shyness, or, inaccessibility.
- A bare window indicates the child is direct, and can often be blunt. Some say if the window has no panes it indicates hostility.
- Curtains covering the window indicate a reserved personality. Curtains also show a concern for beauty at home.
- Lacy curtains or pulled back curtains indicate femininity and again, concern for beauty in the home.
- The four-pane window is the most commonly drawn, but holds no special meaning.
- Many windows indicate a desire for environmental or social contact and a general sense of openness.
- Barred windows indicate a secret the child does not want exposed. Be certain the bars in any interpretation are not meant, by the child, to be windowpanes.

Doors

You know by now that the door to the house represents the interaction with others. The contact between the drawer and his environment.

The lack of a door signals that he is blocking contact with others. He wants to withdraw and may already be inaccessible in many ways. It is a very guarded signal also, in regard to what goes on in his house. But, as I've cautioned with all drawings, you must know something about him and his environment before judging the meaning.

- A large door is a friendly, welcoming symbol. A double door means the same.
- A small door can be a signal of timidity.
- A window in the door emphasizes the comfort of contact with others.
- An open door shows a strong need for social contact. This could mean an unusually powerful need for warmth and approval from others.
- Should there be an additional door sketched on the side of the house it indicates, as you might suspect, that he wants another way out. A means of escape.
- Any door with a crossbar on any type of building, or a complicated lock indicates something private and unrevealed.

The doorknob can bring out the weirdness in some analysts.

To most of us, it is obviously the means by which we open the door, and thereby establish contact on both sides. *It allows the fulfillment of the symbol of the door itself.* A small door missing a doorknob could be drawn by a painfully shy person. A large door without a knob would indicate, to me, a person who needs a lot of contact with others, but isn't receiving it. Does this make sense?

Other analysts have said the doorknob represents dependency. Why? Because it resembles a button (which symbolizes dependency) when drawn in one dimension? Dependency on having contact with others? No, that is symbolized by the door itself.

Some have said the doorknob represents isolation. What does that mean? A *missing* doorknob would better serve any interpretation of isolation.

And others have made me pause, saying it indicates the preoccupation with the phallus! Excuse me? Where in the world does that come from? I must be surrounded by really dull doors.

Common sense must prevail as we weigh one indicator against another in any drawing. Again—the doorknob allows the fulfillment of the symbol of the door itself.

Additions To The House

*   Walkways and steps provide access to the house and are the artist's way of saying "come on in." She is giving you freedom to enter her space.

    A well-proportioned pathway and/or evenly spaced steps are welcoming. The walkway can comfortably turn or wind a bit.

    Be sure to note if there are any obstacles on the path, or if the steps are many or hard to negotiate. This can mean that her basic nature is a welcoming one, but there may be something she is guarding.

    A long pathway with twists and turns presents more difficulty and indicates personal aloofness. If you arrive, fine. If you don't, that is fine too.

*   Bushes, flowers and shrubs growing next to the house provide additional security and grounding.

    They can also represent the number of family members, or the age of the artist, so count them.

*   Fences, garden walls or hedges that surround the house provide a barrier to, and protection from, environmental forces. Either elements in life, or perhaps people.

    When the fence runs from the sides of the house as though enclosing the backyard, but not the front door, the fence becomes more decorative. While it doesn't lose the protective meaning altogether, it is interpreted as less of a barrier.

    The house and the fence in figure 117 provide us a good example of this feature. One of the other things to notice in this nice little house is the canopy over the door. By adding this she enlarges the entrance, though the door itself is comparatively small.

Though she draws neither a base nor a walkway, she anchors the house well with the fence. Then she provides a welcoming window in the door.

It would seem that she is undecided about whether or not she wants the interaction between herself and others, or perhaps her mood will dictate how receptive she is at any specific time.

All of her four-paned windows have feminine, pulled back curtains.

The Person

Somewhere I read a reference that Leonardo da Vinci had observed that the artist will tend to incorporate his own physical form or features into his human drawings. So, it appears to be a trait that is not outgrown.

As you have read here, the person in a drawing of the same age and sex as the artist represents the artist himself. In addition, the child will normally draw his or her own sex, given a free choice of subject.

The exception to this is the adolescent girl. As their interest turns to boys, they often tend to draw male figures of their same general age.

The favored spot on the page is toward the center so the person will often be placed close to, or in, that location. If not, pay attention to what does occupy the middle section of any drawing. Look carefully to see how the person on the page is treated, for example, if there is a barrier or distance between the main person and others or objects in a scene.

When the artist omits himself from a family scene it is significant, and indicates that he feels unimportant. When a known family member is omitted from the group, it can mean a desire on the part of the artist to be rid of him or her, most commonly a sibling. Some children will continue to include a divorced parent with the family group, others will not, or will draw them apart or on the reverse side of the paper. This can tell us a lot about the child's feelings regarding the situation.

Look to see the person by whom the artist places himself. This is the spot in which he feels the safest. Many children, especially those with more than one sibling, simply draw the family in chronological order. The following drawing demonstrates this. Let's look at several things in it.

Figure 124

The 10 year-old sketcher of figure 124 is the fourth of five children. The pressure is very heavy and embossed on the back of the paper. He places himself chronologically second from the left. By now you are knowledgeable enough that several things may leap out at you from this drawing.

While he shows a size difference, all members of the family seem identical. They are a unit in his eyes, with everyone portrayed more or less the same, arms extended to each other. The youngest is a boy; the two sisters and oldest brother are teenagers. You could say that the family comes first with this boy.

Why the open mouths? Any number of reasons. Certainly, in a family of seven each is trying to have his or her own say. An open mouth represents an oral need, which can be food, conversation and/or love. Pointed teeth show some sort of aggression, or even hostility. Mom may be the one to deal with routinely, and all three of the teenagers are periodically put in charge of him. We all know what that's like! Dad and his little brother may be easier to anticipate.

What is missing is always as important as what is included in the sketch. Those fourteen missing feet say that he considers them all to be insecure *in some way* and *as a group.* Feet provide stability, as well as allow mobility, so there is a lack of emotional grounding in this drawing. Do bear in mind, this is his feeling, for his own reasons, and others in the family may not share the same opinion. His feeling could be from a social, financial, emotional cause or any other reason. He portrays himself as even less stable, as he floats higher than the others.

The reluctance to draw feet also suggests a general discouragement, even depression, and is common among those who are physically withdrawn, whether they are bedridden, disabled or simply sedentary.

Another missing feature is the nose on both himself and younger brother. He may feel the older siblings receive more love, nurturing and attention than they do.

I would suggest that this little guy should have help in finding an activity that he can do especially well, and identify as more of his own person than simply an extension of the family group.

Parts Of The Body

It seems useful to view the body in three separate primary sections.

1. The head, neck and facial features, which is the main area of perception, of ego and of self-esteem.
2. The upper body, to include shoulders, arms, hands and the trunk to the waist, which is the physical power area of the human body, and the ability to do for one's self.
3. The lower body, to include the pelvic area, legs and feet, which represents the sexual sphere, security, balance and stability.

1. Head, Neck and Facial Features
Head

Children will usually draw the head of a body first, and it is usually oversized, often until the preteen years. The little fellow in figure 124 has done a good job of sizing the heads to match the bodies, though they are still a bit oversized. The head represents how the child interacts with the rest of the world.

- An oversized head shows a healthy self-esteem, strong intellectual strivings, and/or also a preoccupation with fantasy. It could represent egocentricity based on feelings of inadequacy but this gets complicated for the non-professional.
- A small head may represent feelings of inadequacy, inferiority or an area of painful thoughts or guilt.
- An extreme amount of attention to the hair indicates an adolescent narcissism.

Neck
- The well-proportioned neck shows an acceptance of the body itself.
- A long neck may show a sense of dependency, lack of control, body weakness or a sense of vulnerability.
- A short neck is a dead-giveaway showing stubbornness or even bullheadedness. The person may be extremely impulsive, especially when the neck is thick.
- A missing neck has no meaning in a young child's drawing. If a neck is included but not connected well to the body and/or the head, examine the possible reasons, analyzing what you know about the child.

Face
- A missing face on a drawing will happen from time to time. A young boy presented me with a drawing of his family. I asked why the father had no face...he hurried to add it, saying "I knew I forgot something." He wanted very much to make the addition, so I didn't prevent his doing it. The father was absent from the family much of the time, either at work or asleep. Should the face be missing on a drawing representing the artist, it means a lack of self-acceptance.
- A face drawn in profile may be an experiment in style, but depending on the situation, could be considered evasiveness or even a feeling of guilt. If there are other people or objects in the drawing follow the direction of the gaze to see where it leads.

Eyes
  Eyes reveal the inner person and accompanying feelings.
- Unusually small eyes or slits can mean a tendency toward introversion. A desire to see as little as possible.

- Large eyes, while appearing feminine and innocent, can actually convey suspicion and a hypersensitivity to social situations. Still, there is a desire for social activity and social connection. Large eyes are on the lookout.
- Shaded, heavy eyes betray anxiety.
- Small pupils can show self-absorption. They also reflect a tendency toward contemplation and introspection.
- The "empty eye" with the pupil and/or the iris omitted indicates a desire to not see one's surroundings. The person may be introverted or self-absorbed. This is an eye we do not like to see.
- Eyelashes are a femininity signal, usually drawn by girls.
- A finely drawn eyebrow reflects vanity. Those who draw them spend time on their grooming.
- Heavy, bushy eyebrows drawn over the eye shows a lack of inhibition, and a even certain "gruffness."
- Cockeyed drawings are often done in fun. When a child uses the cross-eyed or goggle-eyed drawing often, it can represent confused thinking. You don't want to see this kind of self-deprecation routinely in a child's drawing.

Nose

The nose is a symbol of both sexuality and the striving for power. The child with allergies will often draw attention to the nose. There are more ways to draw a nose than one can begin to categorize. Let's consider only the basics.

- A button nose is a signal of childish dependency.
- The nose emphasized through heavy pressure or large size shows phallic concern or curiosity.
- A long nose may indicate a sexually outgoing nature.
- A sharp triangular nose or one with emphasis on the nostrils suggests aggression.
- A hooked nose, such as that seen on a witch, is used to represent greed or evil.
- The missing nose addresses a perceived lack of love and nurturing. It can signal low energy or a lack of vitality.

Ears

Missing ears are normal in the sketches of preschool kiddies. Deaf children may draw the ears as either absent or present, and when included, ears are sometimes quite large.

- Always factor in the possibility of a hearing difficulty if the ears are missing, or when drawn large or very small.

- Large or emphasized ears always reflect sensitivity to what others are saying, usually regarding criticism. Very small ears reflect a refusal to listen, usually concerning criticism, or a hearing difficulty
- Missing ears on the older child indicate he chooses not to listen, or is in the habit of not listening, for whatever reason.

Mouth

It is normal for children to draw a wide single-line smile on faces in their sketches. Therefore, in your analysis don't give a lot of credence to a smiling face.

- A slash for a mouth indicates aggressiveness, perhaps hostility, but not necessarily acted out. The same mouth drawn in profile may host a lot of tension.
- A missing mouth shows reluctance to communicate with other people, or possibly depression. Some say it can indicate guilt or rejection of affection. There could be a respiratory condition, or some other disorder.
- An open smiling mouth conveys the sense of oral dependence. This is commonly identified in the earliest psychosexual stage of development when the interest centers on feeding, sucking and biting and progresses as we age to those oral traits of friendliness, generosity, eroticism and don't forget, talkativeness.
- An open mouth with no smile can convey the same as above but to a lesser degree. This mouth suggests oral passivity.
- Visible teeth indicate a tendency to use words in a hostile way or to use sarcasm (they are certainly not the same). The sharper the teeth are drawn, the more "biting" the individual portrayed is likely thought to be.
- The puffy, full-lipped or the cupid's-bow mouth on female figures is associated with sexually precocious adolescent girls.

Chin

- When the chin is emphasized the purpose is to portray dominance in the social world, perhaps in some cases, even aggression.
- If the chin is weak, there is indicated a corresponding social weakness.

- A cleft chin is said by some to indicate strength. It is said by others to be a sign of gender confusion when drawn by a boy on a male figure. I have no sample of a cleft chin in a child's drawing.

2. The Upper Body

The trunk is drawn as a whole by younger children. They will gradually add a suggestion of a waist, if only by clothing. The trunk is the seat of power and drive in the body. The upper portion reflects dominance and physical ability. The waistline is the axis of coordination between the power drive and the sexual drive.

- A large or an angular upper body suggests power.
- A small trunk area may indicate feelings of inadequacy.
- The waist is emphasized by girls to show femininity.
- The reluctance to draw the body from the waist down can be a signal of sexual disturbance.

Shoulders

- The power center of the body. Large, squared shoulders suggest aggressive tendencies, or in the case of young artists, they are often just trying to make a figure look masculine.
- Erasures and reinforcements to shoulders indicates a preoccupation with the strivings for physical power.
- Noticeably uneven or unbalanced shoulders indicate an emotional instability.
- Small shoulders can equate to feelings of inferiority.

Arms and Hands

These appendages allow us to demonstrate our manual, as well as our physical, contact with the environment.

- Missing arms show a sense of helplessness, or a general dissatisfaction or depression.
- Very short arms may indicate withdrawal, and an absence of striving or lack of ambition.
- Long arms show either a need for contact, or an acquisitiveness. There may be a demand for affection or striving for success.
- Muscular arms with strong shoulders show an aggressive drive for power.
- Weak, thin or limp arms show, as you might suspect, an inadequacy or physical weakness.

- Arms behind the back show a social reluctance. There can also be guilt or feelings of hostility concealed.
- Arms folded across the chest show suspicion.
- Arms on the hips show an in-charge "bossiness." The artist may be narcissistic.
- Hands hidden behind the back or in pockets indicate a lack of confidence and an unwillingness to confront a specific situation or new situations in general
- Unusually large hands are considered aggressive by some, and impulsive by others.
- A large thumb is a phallic symbol.
- If the hands or fingers are shaded in any way the interpretation is one of guilt...theft, masturbation, etc.
- Hands and/or arms are often missing from the figure in a normal drawing of a young child, but when missing from the drawing of a more mature person *can* indicate a sense of inadequacy or guilt.
- Fingers convey mood and message and are easily read. The more pointed they are, the more aggressive or hostile the intent. Spikes drawn of single lines are considered infantile. Rounded fingers are gentle unless they form a rebellious fist.

Figure 125

The boy who drew figure 125 has demonstrated that his friend to the right, who is a girl, may be smaller than he (at least in his expression) but is his equal. The little girl defined by name, is a known social leader in their group. Notice that her shoulders are, in proportion to the size he has made her, just as powerful as his.

Hands and feet are not yet included in his drawing repertoire. The right arm of the girl may be portrayed in a more gentle fashion to show that she is stroking her cat.

3. The Lower Body

The lower trunk is the sexual sphere. This seat of our human drive and activity and can prove to be a puzzle for the child until she figures out how to treat it.

The pelvic area is often ignored or treated as the continuation of the trunk oval, or the legs on a man will be drawn from the bottom of the trunk oval, or attached to the waist, all of which is normal. The female form is easier to clothe, disguise and forget about.

About the time the youngster starts school (and contends with all the elements of a new education), or begins including waistlines on her figures, or happens to see her dad or a brother without the full complement of clothing, she becomes "handicapped" by new additions to the artwork.

A reluctance of the drawer to close the bottom of the trunk oval should be considered a sexual preoccupation. A temporary problem of how to draw the lower body for one child, can be a whole new way of thinking for another.

Look what happened to the unsuspecting artist of the next figure on the following page. The little girl who drew figure 126 decided to make her drawing conform a little more to what she knew was real.

She had been doing just fine with her use of a single trunk oval. Then she added another oval below (seen with a light) in order to depict the lower body, known to exist, just as the leg transparency does.

When the new drawing experiment went sour for her she wanted to eliminate it. How could she do that? With *shading*, which not only crossed out the new oval but also showed her frustration regarding the whole effort. Shading, remember, always indicates some degree of anxiety.

Figure 126

You must always know what you are looking at. This drawing with the shading covering the genitals could be interpreted as something much more serious without information about the family, the origin of the drawing and the intention of the child.

She'll gradually work this out with another stage of drawing, involving pants of some sort, with a waist or a shirt arrangement. If she were to ignore the lower body and continue to draw the youthful trunk, it would in effect show a denial of human drive and impulse, or express feelings of inferiority.

Pelvic Area and Legs

- Because the area below the waist is the sexual sphere of the body, a large belt or a tightly cinched belt draws attention to sexual tension. There may be some difficulty between expression and control of impulses.
- When the pants and pant legs are shaded in a drawing it portrays some sort of sexual anxiety. This can be as simple (with boys) as comparing oneself to a brother or father. It can also be a more serious situation.
- If the entire figure slants and the leg (or legs) seems to float into the air, there is dependency or instability.
- Very long legs show autonomy and independence. Or a striving for autonomy.
- Short legs convey a feeling of lack of mobility.
- Legs drawn tightly together depict rigidity and tension. This can portray a holding back of sexual energy.
- Crossed legs are a defense against any sexual approach.
- A very wide stance is considered aggressive, especially when the figure occupies the center of the paper.

Feet

Legs and feet together provide stability, of course. A person needs solid footing. Feet are often considered phallic, especially when analyzing drawings by adolescent males. It is also interesting to note that girls of all ages will embellish their drawings of shoes in a feminine way. A foot in a shoe is a phallic symbol.

- Omission of feet is always a sign of discouragement, perhaps depression, and a signal of insecurity. The child needs grounding in some way.
- Very small feet may indicate constriction, certainly some insecurity and dependence. Many times you will see tiny feet shaded as though to give them added stability. The drawers of tiny feet maintain rigid sexual control.
- A figure standing on tiptoe should give you pause for thought. Look at other indicators in the drawing for confirmation, because this always indicates a loose grip on reality and a tendency toward fantasy. (Naturally, be certain the drawing isn't depicting a thief or a ballerina.)
- Very long feet show strong security needs and can show concern over gender identity. When very long shoes with

crossed shoelaces are drawn by adolescent boys it supposedly indicates castration fears.

- Very large feet show the need for grounding and security; when exaggerated, even in a comedic way, they can be considered phallic.

Sexual Symbols

Open portrayal of the sexual organs in drawings is still considered taboo in our society. Children instinctively know this and usually refrain from including bare breasts or a vulva or a penis in a drawing. When a penis, is included in the drawing of a young child it will have to be explained, excused or "alibied," if not turned over to Social Services in some cases. Try to handle it, please, should a child present you with a precise drawing someday.

This is not to say that symbols are used as conscious substitutes for the real thing. All use of symbolism is on a subconscious level.

Both males and females use sexual symbols. Girls are curious once they've noticed the differences between male and female anatomy. And boys, judging from my experience as a female and a mom, are constantly reminded because of their troublesome, erratic body part which seems to have a mind of its own.

Perhaps the easiest symbol to identify is the male phallus. Phallic symbols are only those resembling the penis, not sexual symbols in general.

I refer you once more to figure 51 in chapter three. The house is very unusual and a phallic symbol, but not all tall houses are considered so; you can see the difference. This analysis is reinforced by the shading from the waist down on the boy, signaling sexual anxiety.

Be cautious interpreting sexual symbols. Each of us comes from a unique background, armed with an original personality and a variety of compulsions, and so do these children. We can identify the symbol but we cannot say *why* it is there.

Again, the more you know about the child and his situation, the better you can understand the drawing. Don't put a lot of stress on sexuality in a child's sketch, just learn to recognize some basics. Remember, sexual interest is a major component of the human condition.

Sexual symbols are far too numerous to include all, so a couple of "rules to live by" can serve us well. In general the phallic shape is considered male (no revelation here) and any type of container that can hold liquid, or contain objects is considered female, as are circular objects. Water is always feminine. Elongated fish in the water are masculine. (Suddenly the image of Dustin Hoffman starring in *"The Graduate"* floating on his raft in the pool comes to mind...a perfect example of visual sexual symbolism...as those of us old enough to remember can attest.)

Bananas and dates are considered masculine while figs and pomegranates are feminine, fertile symbols loaded with seeds. Any boat on the surface is feminine, but the huge prow, but *only* the prow, that you see on a Viking ship is masculine. Submarines, however, are always considered to be masculine. Don't kill the messenger, I'm only reporting, not originating the data. Consult a book of symbols for a further adventure.

Figure 127

Remember these images cropped from figure 60? The phallic shark is chasing a phallic submarine which is firing phallic torpedoes. Whew, I've always suspected it's tough being a boy.

And this is my point exactly. Why wouldn't you find an abundance of phallic symbols in the world of little guys who are forced by nature to live in a phallic world?

In figure 128 drawn by another 7 year-old, we again see the elongated fish, the eel, and another submarine, somewhat cramped, probably an afterthought. The keyhole in the treasure chest is not really a sexual symbol without the key being present. Dad is safely waiting inside the boat at the top of the drawing, according to the artist.

Figure 128 (53)

Figure 129

Do little girls ever draw phallic symbols in their pictures? Probably not as often as boys, but certainly just as blatantly when they do. These next three drawings, done by girls, are worth examining.

In figure 129 the 9 year-old child shows the sexual curiosity that goes with her age, and a new baby in the family serves to reinforce the wonder. The prominence of the bottle and nipple is not coincidental. The stress on the detail of the father's fly can be interpreted also as a flaccid penis. She incorporates all this interest into the normal course of daily activity.

The girl who drew figure 130 is a young teen. How many symbols do we need in one place before we notice her budding interest in sex? We have the phallic symbols of the shark, as well as the foot in the high-heeled shoe. The balance of the page is covered with sexual oval and circular figures. The most interesting character to me is the one by the shoe. It displays both male and female features which means nothing, but further shows her experimentation of the moment with all things sexual.

Figure 130

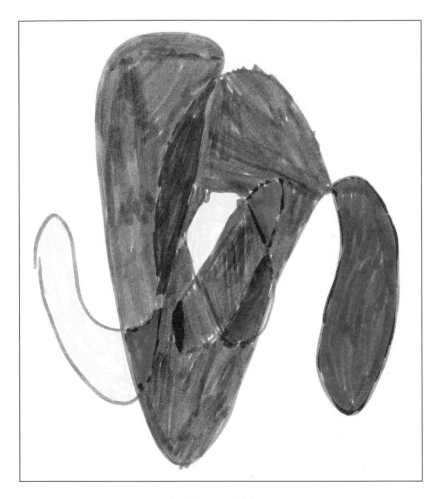

Figure 131

Believe me, the 7½ year-old girl who drew figure 131 sees only a nicely colored, embellished heart shape. She would be horrified to know that an adult can see both male and female sexual organs. She's in the process of learning about all this tricky adult stuff, whether she wants to or not, but certainly doesn't want you to know that she has much interest. Never embarrass a child by pointing these things out to them. "Tell me about your pretty heart," must be your only comment.

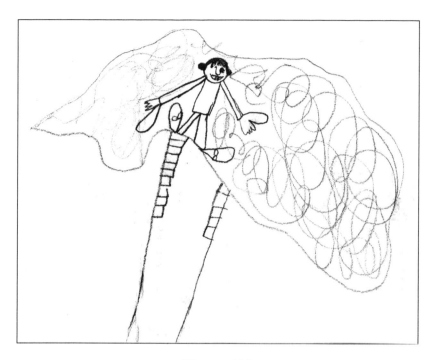

Figure 132

We are back to boys, can you tell? The artist of this "listening activity" from school was approximately 10 years old when he drew figure 132, and we can see he was listening primarily to his hormones. Mothers everywhere, do not despair; I know the family of this boy and he grew up just fine in spite of the fact that he has five (including the nose) phallic symbols displayed on his body. It is worth noting how he has also emphasized his ears as he draws and listens to the music.

His hormones may literally have him a little off base, as the drawing lists decidedly into the masculine area. He is firmly grounded in his tree however. We'll see him again.

As I've said before, I have little patience with those analysts who dwell on the presence of phallic symbols as something abnormal and unexpected. There are definite ways of drawing that can tweak you to something wrong in a child's life, which we'll touch on in a later chapter, but an expression of sexual symbols is normal.

Figure 133

The 10 year-old boy who drew figure 133 refers to "making out" as "nasty." Can you tell? Look first at the two phallic swings and the single female sexual symbol in the tire swing. The subject of sex is very much on his mind.

He has the entire symbol secured on a double ground line and placed in the middle of a raging storm, complete with the word "lightning" written twice. He doesn't know how to deal with the emotion.

This child acquires his limited and apparently biased sexual knowledge from older children, no doubt. He displays an obvious interest in sexual matters, and could use some responsible input from parents or other sources.

One encouraging symbol? The clouds are neither dark nor threatening.

A male friend of mine commented on the subject of sexual signals, "I'm not sure I believe all that."

My amused response was the same as the one the reincarnationist gave to the agnostic, "In the end it doesn't matter whether you believe it or not."

Chapter Six
The Tree Drawing

"I like trees because they seem more resigned
to the way they have to live than other things do."
Willa Cather

There is neither a good tree drawing nor a bad tree drawing. The tree we draw shows where we are in our life experience and how we have handled it all so far. We even draw different trees at different times.

Try to remember how you drew a tree as a child; better yet, take out a piece of paper and draw the tree. Now, on the back or on a fresh piece of paper, draw the tree you feel like drawing today. If you don't do this now, before you learn more, you will wish you had. C'mon, reward yourself.

Let's take the mystery out of the drawings by going to the gut-level feel of the sketch. You will discover a certain accuracy in your reaction. These composites are by adults.

Figure 134

In figure 134, which drawing reflects depression opposed to a feeling of low self-esteem? You probably correctly selected the drawing on the right. Trust yourself to feel it.

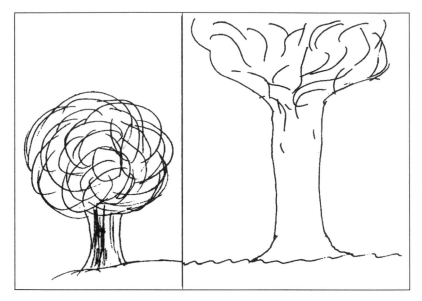

Figure 135

Which tree in figure 135 conveys aspiration and enthusiasm? Which tree refuses to top-out and settle for where it is? Which tree says "lemme outta here?" The tree on the right, of course. There is nothing wrong with the tree on the left. It's a contented little tree, happy in itself. The one on the right was drawn by a person who expects more of himself and may see an opportunity to make it happen.

Both of the trees in figure 136 have been drawn by caring, intelligent, fun-loving women. One is a 19 year-old college student who lives at home and has a steady boyfriend. The other is a 45 year-old straight-commission saleswoman who is the only source of income for herself and her child. Can you sense the difference?

You're correct if you feel the younger woman drew the tree on the right. The conifer belongs to the older woman.

Figure 136

Any conifer is a goal-oriented tree, appearing almost like an arrowhead, going straight up. There is the goal of income and security, in addition to any others, on the mind of the older woman. The college student was complaining as she drew it that her tree, on your right, looked like a flower. Without analyzing the girl's tree, we can draw an analogy. Certainly she is in a very maturing, flowering and flirtatious period in her life and the tree reflects this.

Tree Symbolism

The tree has universal significance for us and it is symbolically woven through cultures around the world. It manifests earthly roots, contact with waters and branches reaching toward the heavens, forming an *axis mundi,* or a world axis. The tree is a feminine representation of the sheltering, nourishing symbolism of The Great Mother.

Buddha found enlightenment under the Bodhi tree, Adam and Eve fell from grace at the Tree of Knowledge. Christ is shown crucified on a tree in Medieval paintings. Muslim faithful pray on carpets woven with the Tree of Life and Odin sacrificed himself on the Yggdrasil, the Scandanavian Cosmic Tree. Egyptians held the acacia tree sacred.

Traditionally the hammer handle of a Freemason is made of beech wood to signify endurance, and followers of Germanic tribes worship in oak groves, still. Cypress trees, thought to preserve bodies, are planted in cemeteries, still, and the tree-based fertility rite of the maypole dance is practiced, still.

Whether we consider cultures of the world or fictional works, the symbolism of the tree is present in mythologies throughout the world.

In the love story of Tristan and Isolde, the two trees planted on their graves entwine. And who knows how many cartoon characters have run for their lives through primeval forests, barely escaping the clutching branches of huge black trees gone bad.

There are seemingly endless references to the tree, whether represented as a coniferous evergreen tree or a leafy deciduous one, with its yearly growth, loss and regeneration.

Is it any wonder that one of the first images the child draws is that of the tree?

Tests...Briefly

There are systems you may have heard of for testing intelligence and/or personality based on drawings, such as the House-Tree-Person Test (H-T-P) by John Buck, the Draw A Man test by Goodenough, the Draw A Person (DAP) test by Machover and others. These are based on participation by the clinician and are subjective in many cases. Go carefully if investigating various interpretations as one may be led astray by lists of often conflicting traits. We are not testing, we are reading signals already completed on paper, and weighing them against one another, as well as known facts regarding the artist.

I have the highest regard for Dr. Karen Bolander's information in her book *Assessing Personality Through Tree Drawings*. Her method is based heavily on the teachings of a Hungarian priest, Father Károly Ábel, a psychologist and educator.

The Tree And Its Parts

Why am I so smitten with a tree drawing as an interpretive vehicle? It is much easier for everyone to draw a tree, rather than a person for a variety of reasons, and feelings can be projected into a tree drawing that cannot be expressed otherwise, possibly because it is perceived as a neutral entity. We are able to see how the artist relates to his environment.

Those analysts who claim the tree drawing to be the person *himself* are wrong, in my opinion. The tree is the projection of *the individual's subconscious feelings about himself,* a reflection of what he has experienced in life and, in some instances, his anticipation of the future.

Carl Jung said (in paraphrase) that if the mandala is the symbol for the cross section of the self, then the tree drawing represents the profile view of the self, seen as a process of growth.

When you have a drawing of a tree alone you can best assess the priority of placement on the page. Placement applies for a tree as well as a person. Quite often the child doesn't plan where to put the tree but adds it as she draws. Yet, you can often tell that the drawing started with the tree even with other objects present. Refer again to figure 8 and notice the three vertical spheres of the page. The lower is instinctual, the middle is emotional, reflecting how one interacts with others, and the upper is mental.

The tree is also comprised of three sections—roots, trunk and crown—and regardless of where it is drawn on the page, each section of the tree maintains its own meaning, which is the same as those in the spheres of the page. The root area represents the instinctual, the trunk is an expression of emotion relating to environment and the crown represents all things mental, often including goals.

Look at the entire tree before examining the sections or any additions such as animals or nests.

The vertical axis of the tree is also a timeline. The bottom of the tree, whether roots or base, is viewed as the infancy of the artist's life and the top of the crown as the current age.

Some maintain that chronological events can be tracked on the tree, especially traumas, by the method of measuring the tree. Divide the height of the tree to arrive at half the age of the person and proceed in this divisional way to check against scars or knotholes and other indicators. Try it for yourself with known examples if you care to, but I do not depend on this methodology.

Because many folks do not draw a root system and others draw the tree crown flowing off the top of the page, it seems unreliable to me. But should you be interested, Dr. Bolander's book has a much more complicated formula.

Let's take a look at the tree drawings of children only, from this point on, to see how they differ from adult drawings and what they have in common with each other.

Figure 137

Here in figure 137 you see a composite of trees drawn by kids from age 6 to age 13. Just for the record, one girl, one boy and one tomboy.

You can quickly see the commonalties. Missing root systems, the dominant trunk length and small crowns are universal traits in the drawings of young children. Also normal is the marked division between crown and trunk.

Why? Because they are emotional beings with still unreliable instincts and developing mental skills.

The trees of children can be analyzed well, but not in the detail reserved for the tree of an adult. The child is a work in progress of course, without a great deal of life experience. Though a child may draw many styles of trees, they will usually have certain dimensions in common.

For the record, the 13 year-old boy included a flower by the tree and the 9 year-old tomboy drew the middle tree.

The Crown

Here is the mental arena. We see how one's thought is influenced and how it becomes processed and applied. Crown styles are abundant. Notice first if the outside of the crown is closed by a line or a series of lines, or if it is open, with numerous branch endings. The crown may be bare or foliated; it may contain fruit. Notice also the relative size of the crown to the trunk. Does the crown have a prominent side, or does it list to one side, or is it balanced?

The crown will have what I call an attitude. It may have an appearance of being stationary, such as the closed "cloud" crowns in figure 138, or the open crown of a winter tree, similar to the one in figure 139. Or the crown may appear to be heading in an upward direction like a conifer, a yew, or a poplar. It may also be heading downward in the form of a weeping willow or birch. Some palm trees are portrayed in a downward mode.

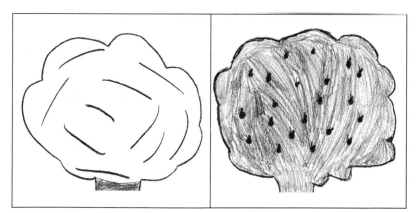

Figure 138

The closed crown like those in figure 138 is perhaps the most common style crown, meant to portray the leafy deciduous tree, often with no branches showing. The drawer of the closed crown is mentally very self-contained, that is to say, not dependent on others for mental stimulation nor necessarily receptive to outside influences, though they are usually friendly people. While being very self-sufficient, they also have a need to remove outside contacts in order to accomplish their own creative projects.

Figure 139

The open crown can take different forms but that of the winter deciduous tree in figure 139 is rather common.

The 14 year-old artist of this open crown is receptive to influences of his environment and can assimilate and control the stimulation. His branch ends are closed.

The artist of the same age in figure 140 will have a little more trouble because the ends of the branches are wide open and he may, consequently, be inundated with stimulus from his environment. Each is an extrovert in his own way.

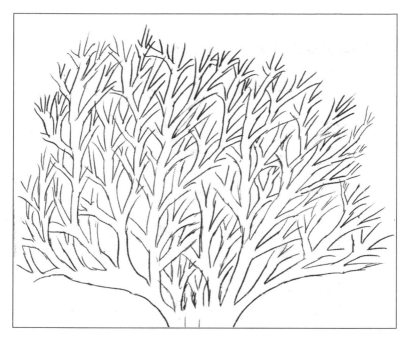

Figure 140

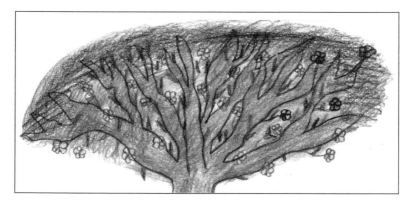

Figure 141

What have we here in figure 141? A masquerade of a closed crown pretending to be open. Close examination shows it to be completely colored with green crayon and darkly covered along the entire canopy. This type of shading forms a closed crown without a defined outside line, and closes what started as an open-branched crown. The artist wants to keep most aspects of her mental activity secret. She may not feel capable of dealing with challenges. She may have mother issues, or she may be very self-indulgent.

You may notice the branches have a pincer-like quality. What you feel is correct, there is a hostile aggression present in this young teen that can manifest at any time. While the flowers could be simple adornment of the crown, they may well be sweet decoys, in this instance, for her underlying aggression.

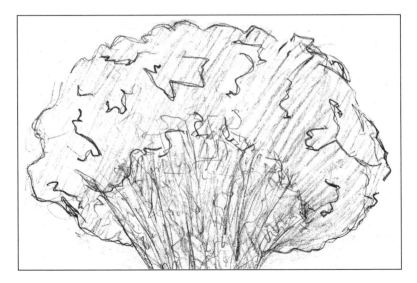

Figure 142

The crown in figure 142 appears to be closed but look at all the openings along the outside edge, coupled with the abundance of branches emerging from the trunk. This is a semi-open crown. The foliage only appears solid and closed, therefore we have a happy medium between the self-imposed containment of the closed crown and the free flow of the open crown to and from outside influences.

The crowns in figure 143 are also representations of the semi-open crown. The suggestion of foliage by squiggles shows a more active mental life than an empty crown does.

Figure 143

Below in figure 144 is a beautiful example of the filtered, open crown, with some branch ends open and others closed. The leaves provide the filtering system that allows the artist to protect himself from outside influence. A flexible, friendly sort of buffer zone from which to choose the extent of his interaction with outside contacts.

Figure 144

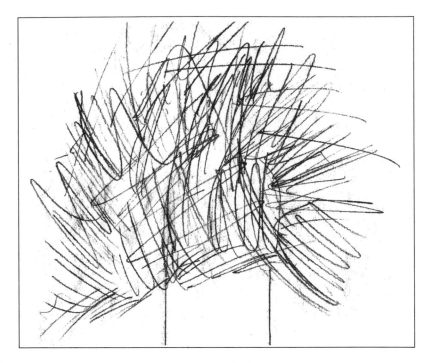

Figure 145

Foliage suggested by a loose line shading done with the tip of the pencil, without an outside line, such as figure 145, may show an inability to release energy consistently. But the absence of an outside line on the crown always indicates an ability to interact openly with the environment.

The loose shading in figure 146 is another form of scribbled crown also done with the tip of the pencil, rather than the side of the lead. The circular motion changes the meaning to one of self-involvement related to ego. This artist will carefully analyze her own interests when interacting with her environment.

The single-stroke branches show a direct approach to any activity in which she chooses to participate.

The end point of any branch represents the contact between the self and others in the environment, as you have seen by these various explanations.

Figure 146

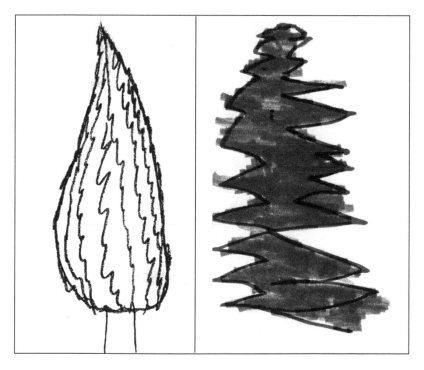

Figure 147

In figure 147 you see the attitude of upward moving crowns. The poplar or similar tree drawers with the upward moving branches are always mentally dominated and move consistently toward their goals, usually in an optimistic way. When trying to appeal to their feelings, be sure to take the logical approach.

The drawers of the coniferous pine are just as goal oriented but must take the project step by step. They may be deeply emotional, but are also vulnerable and suspicious. They are hard workers, not easily distracted and are quite stubborn. These folks are sensitive and can have their feelings hurt in spite of their appearance of self-confidence.

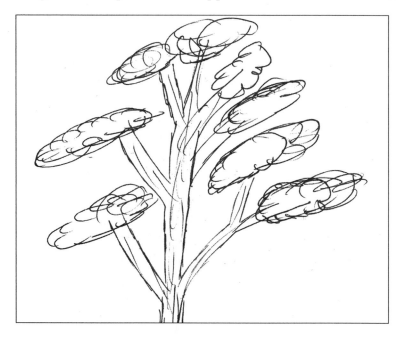

Figure 148

The Oriental cedar shown in figure 148 with its pretty puffs of foliage is a true conifer but more openly structured.

The drawer, though still goal oriented and moving ambitiously ahead, may be juggling so many projects that he will have to abandon some, often due to boredom. Rarely disappointed, these likeable cedar folks can move on to other things easily. Think *resilience* when you see a cedar.

Figure 149

The dead crown of figure 149 is not found often in the drawings of children. The artist of this one was in his early teens, and may have drawn it simply for the effect. If done seriously, the artist may feel victimized and will have a tendency to blame anyone or anything but himself, for his feelings of hopelessness.

In the early decades of the twentieth century when few analysts were around and knowledge was sparse, the meaning evolved that trees with a downward attitude indicated depression. This is usually not the case.

We now know that branches and limbs folding down onto the trunk, such as a willow tree, are drawn often by folks who are reluctant to be approached directly. They can be approached successfully through their emotions, but don't let this fool you. These are thinking folks and the mind will rule ultimately. The branches flow over the trunk, but are still representative of the crown, the mental sphere.

Figure 150 and figure 151 show this type of crown. This is the first time you have seen a crown with an open top and it leads to interesting vulnerabilities.

Figure 150

Older willow artists are open to influences from "above." This can take the form of superstition, religious illumination or fantasy "knowledge" of all sorts. It results from the blending of the mental crown with the emotional sphere of the trunk, and it is typical of even the most intelligent of those who routinely draw willows.

The leaves or buds on the ends of the branches in figure 151 show a belief that whatever is happening in the present is bound to get better, or will end well.

Notice both artists shown in figure 152 have tried to close the tops of the willows. They instinctively recognize and resist the wide open top. I gave up attempts to draw this tree crown as a child, because the open top bothered me.

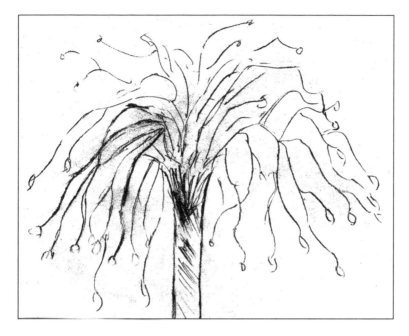

Figure 151

Figure 152

The palm is similar to the willow though the crown is naturally small compared to the tall trunk. Still, the top is open. While the willow folks are *passive* receivers, the palm drawers may be active *instigators* of psychic or inspirational information. Mature palm artists are excitement seekers, yet when challenged by any new adventure, or a strange person, they can revert quickly to a defensive posture.

They are emotionally based and not easily swayed by logical argument. This meshes, because of the small, open crown and the long expanse of the emotion-based trunk.

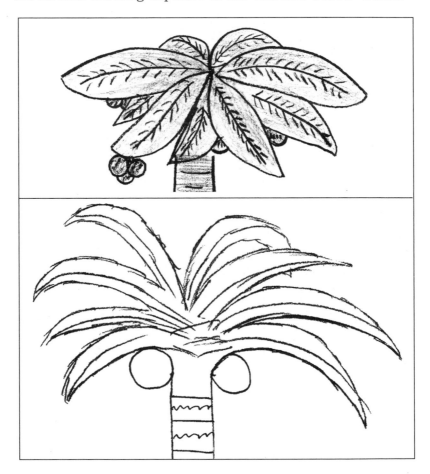

Figure 153

And, as in the case of the willow crowns, you see in figure 154 two successful but unnatural-looking attempts to close the tops of these palm crowns.

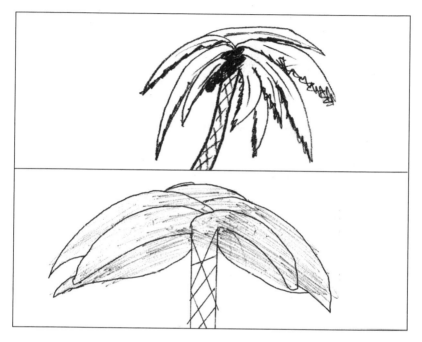

Figure 154

Transition To The Trunk

The point at which the crown meets the trunk shows the integration between the artist's mental life and the emotional responses.

This is categorized in one of three possible ways, regardless of the type of tree: (1) the closed connection, showing a separating line or the bottom of the crown forming a solid line, (2) the partially closed connection, showing the trunk opening into the crown in places, or (3) the open connection, showing the trunk flowing into the crown without a division.

Why is this important to analyze? We find our clues here as to the way the personality will express itself, and how the emotions may be displayed.

In figure 137 we saw the typical style of the younger child's tree drawing. Look again at the transition points from crown to trunk in this blowup in figure 155.

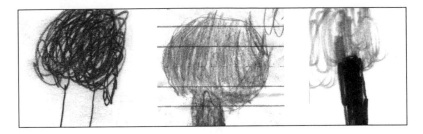

Figure 155

The foliage in all cases is a different color than the trunk, forming a closed connection. In the center crown the child has drawn a black line to separate them further.

Most children start off in this fashion because there is a distinct separation between the emotional and the mental and the emotional rules. They are learning control, with a little luck, and a lot of adult guidance. There is a conscious effort to keep feelings under control.

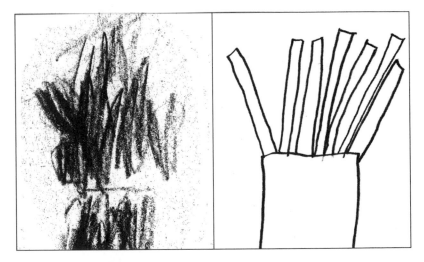

Figure 156

We see other styles of closed crowns in figure 156. The scribbled crown on the left is separated even further by space, as well as by the line. He may well have been severely disciplined for an emotional response.

The stump-like example on the right may be drawn by very young kids, showing there is not much of importance going on mentally yet.

Those who draw the partially closed connection such as those in figures 157, and 142, as well as the willow representations, are trying to gain more control of their emotions. They may even be trying to conceal emotion, or feel they are unsuccessful in doing so.

Figure 157

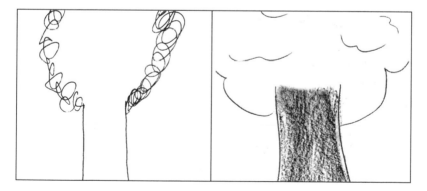

Figure 158

The open transition to the crown allows the feelings from the emotional sphere to mingle freely with the thought process. It also allows mental energy to influence emotion.

A balanced exchange is the ideal, of course. We see two examples of the open transition in figure 158. The transition on the left is the most typical and simply shows the open exchange. When the trunk penetrates a large, fully developed crown as in the drawing on the right, you know the mental processes will be influenced by emotion.

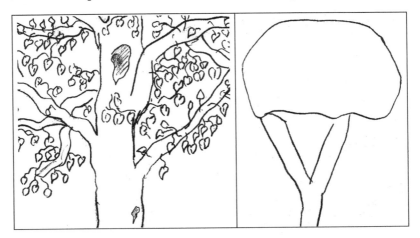

Figure 159

Here on the left side of figure 159 you see the trunk flowing into the crown containing many open branches. This boy will bring good energy and balanced emotion into many aspects of life.

On the right is a common division of the trunk into two main branches where the crown actually begins before they connect to the foliage. This demonstrates two equal areas of interest and development.

The Trunk

We've touched on the dominance of the trunk in the young child's drawing. In addition to being the seat of emotional interaction, the trunk also channels the energy of life. As anyone who spends time with a young child can tell you, they certainly go together.

As the child ages and develops social skills and mental capacity, the trunk length comes more into balance with the crown of the tree, which becomes larger. The child's emotional function remains the same but the ability to relate internally to the emotions matures.

Early analysts felt that the ego resided in the trunk. Many today believe that the entire tree better represents, as stated before, the subconscious feelings regarding the self.

In your explorations you may find analysts who feel the length of the trunk represents the goals of the subject. I fail to see how that explains the extreme length on the trunk of the youngster. Stick with those of us who place goals and aspirations where they belong...at the top of the crown.

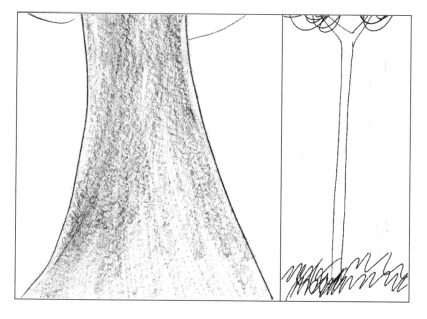

Figure 160

Here you have in figure 160 two extremes in the size of the tree trunks. The length is more or less equal but the difference in width is impressive. If the trunk is the indicator of emotional dominance does this illustration on the right mean the subject lacks emotion? No, the difference is, in part, the way in which one brings emotion to the surface, to the environment, and how much emotion is invested.

The drawer of the slender trunk will have subtle or sensitive responses, and may not have the depth of emotion which is present in those who draw a wider trunk. This person would never be involved, of her own accord, in an emotional confrontation. The very slender trunk topped by a small crown (other than a natural depiction of a palm tree) however, reflects a shallowness of emotional response.

The trunk on the left in figure 160 is drawn by a 14 year-old with extreme sensitivity and emotional depth, a common trait among teens. We wouldn't want to see the trunk any wider however, and it may trim down as time passes and the subject ages.

The extremely broad trunk in relationship to the whole tree, such as that in figure 161 is not healthy. It reflects a sloppy sort of sentimentality and emotional self-indulgence rather than depth of feeling. Can you see how this could translate to some analysts as ego? Certainly all emotion revolves around and relates to the self in this case.

Figure 161

Most of the trees we see in drawings will have trunks that are between these extremes of size, indicating the normal range of emotional response and depth of feeling. Let's look at some of the shapes we routinely encounter.

Remember, the trunk is the vehicle for the flow of energy between the instinctual sphere toward the root area and the mental sphere of the crown.

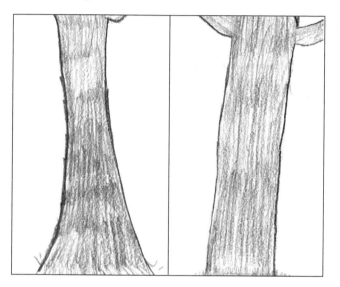

Figure 162

These shapes in figure 162 are the most common that pre-teen and adolescent children draw. They may be slightly shaded as these are to represent bark, or simply outlined. They may be somewhat wider or more narrow.

We like to see a comfortable openness and flow throughout the trunk and these are both positive examples.

The trunk on your left shows a widening toward the lower section, and a slight widening again as it enters the crown. This artist accepts and utilizes feelings, somehow understanding that they represent a harmonious connection between instincts and consciousness.

The straighter trunk on the right also has a good flow of energy between the two but the artist may be slightly more reserved or formal in expressing emotion.

The next examples might be drawn in a similar way as those in figure 162, yet they are totally different.

The widening in both places in the trunk on the left in figure 163 is exaggerated to the point of being like a funnel. The center part of the trunk is constricted and may not be able to process the input from the mental and the instinctual spheres. The flow is hampered, much like many lanes on a freeway trying to merge into a lane or two.

Figure 163

The tree trunk on the right has been drawn with a ruler, as has the limb, and then colored in. The 8 year-old boy who drew it is full of emotion but quite reserved about expressing it. He can pull back to an emotionally "safe" position very quickly, doesn't want to make mistakes, and especially does not want to be chastised for them. He is not an emotional risk-taker. Try to encourage a child like this draw without the ruler.

Continue to be aware of the pressure used in a tree drawing and the steadiness of the strokes. Notice if there is pressure coming from one side or another (figure 8) which will bend the trunk in the *opposite* direction. Pay attention to obvious bulges in the trunk and on which side one might appear. This affects the flow of emotion and the balance between the spheres. It will take some practice to make sense of all these signals but knowing the personality of a child and the life circumstance will confirm what you see.

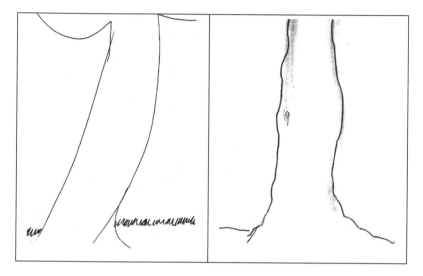

Figure 164

The trunk on the left in figure 164 shows you the child feels pressure from the mother, or another close female relative. (You see the same pressure on the trunk in figure 136.) Look at the direct stroke that makes the left side of the trunk. The drawer reconnects with a straight stroke up to the crown, after realizing the abrupt angle. Seeing the precarious position at the base of the tree, he adds balance on the right. The trunk originates left of center. He is trying to identify with the masculine side.

A bulge on the trunk should be viewed as a "clog" of emotion. The bulge in the trunk on the right is on the father side of the trunk. The tree is drawn toward the left of center. An argument can be made that there are also enlargements on the left. I would say this boy has been hurt emotionally by, or because of, both parents. He sympathizes more with the mother but has a great deal of emotion invested in his dad. A bulge is seen as a longing or a search for approval.

In an older person it might pertain to a romantic interest, but with children I am convinced this clogging of emotion regards the parents or parental figures.

Figure 165

When the trunk changes direction two or more times it creates a wave-like formation, indicating a subject who is malleable and can be easily influenced. You see this in figure 165, but also note that the crown is a willow. With the crown open to influences from "above," you have the type that an Irish friend of mine calls "a wee bit airy-fairy." Fortunately the wave-form emotion is usually optimistic and positive.

Figure 166

The trunk in figure 166 divides well before it reaches the crown area. When you see this you can be certain that the emotion of the drawer is strongly divided between two important areas. This can reflect loyalty to both divorced parents, for instance, or equal emotion involving two completely separate and perhaps opposed interests.

Should the twin trunks cross each other the conflicting interests will be invested with deep emotion, and not easily resolved.

Trunk Base, Root And Ground

This area would contain an enormous amount of information in the same section for an adult reference, but far less for our younger subjects. Why should this be so?

The lower sphere harbors and contributes to our instincts, our physicality which includes sexuality, and our past experience as it relates to daily practicality and related memory. All are still-developing or subjugated traits in our youngster.

The young child who acts on his base instincts, for instance, and decides to take a bite out of a playmate finds himself in the middle of a "time-out" if he's lucky, or examining his mom's teeth prints on his arm (through his tears) if he is not. Now his basic instinct is adjusted and contributes to practical memory.

The root system itself gives clues in an adult drawing to the sexual attitudes. But in regard to children, though sexual interest blossoms continually, in the normal and protected childhood there is no actual experience of any consequence to draw on (pun intended). If a child routinely draws roots he may be introspective and unusually curious.

Let's not forget that in reality the tree roots are not routinely visible, so the child trying for realism in a sketch will not include them. I see more adult tree drawings without a root system than with one, so it seems the tendency to draw only that which can be seen continues.

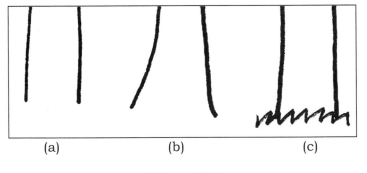

(a)   (b)   (c)

Figure 167

The most common treatments of the base of the tree meeting the ground are shown in figure 167. The majority of kids, regardless of age, seem to use a variation of these three. Examples (a) and (b) are both open to the instinctual influences and can be found anywhere on a page with the bottom wide open. Some will ground an open tree at the bottom edge of the paper but it is still considered wide open. As the bottom flares in (b) the middle sketch, the drawer recognizes the need for a better, more stabilized contact with the instinctual influence.

The grass in figure 167 (c) shows the artist is aware of the influence, possibly sexual, and "protects" himself with a filter in the same manner the leaves do in the crown of a tree. He will easily learn from past experience.

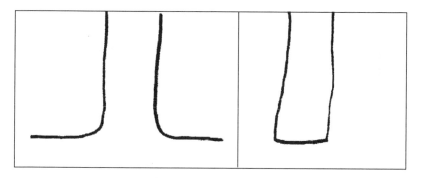

Figure 168

The same thing is happening in these examples in figure 168, though these are not common treatments. On your left the drawer recognizes that he needs stabilization to deal with these influences so he incorporates the ground into the tree base. On the right you see the line included straight across the base of the tree. He will block his instincts in order to deal with them, at least for the time being.

The trunk with a more or less flat ground line under or around it holds no particular meaning.

When the tree is placed on an uphill slope as at the left of figure 169 it shows the drawer believes he can use his environment to get ahead and is an optimist. If the drawing were placed to the left of the page however, it could indicate that something has to be overcome regarding the mother or the future has a large obstacle in the artist's path.

Figure 169

The conifer on the right side is on a slippery slope, showing us the sketcher is wary or insecure, probably about something looming in the near future.

Figure 170

The artist who places her tree on a knoll or a rise feels superior to her peers. This is vanity based and may not be the result of any real skill or accomplishment.

Figure 171

A lone tree placed toward the edge of a hill or on a mountain, similar to what we see in figure 171, can have one of two meanings. Again, if you know something about the drawer the interpretation may be easy. Ambition to succeed or achieve is the most common meaning, but a sense of isolation is the other, and cannot be ruled out. In fact, if an individual works so hard to achieve that he sacrifices the company of friends, couldn't it mean both?

The suggestion of roots here in figure 172 is subtle, and one of the few examples you may begin see in the drawings of adolescent children.

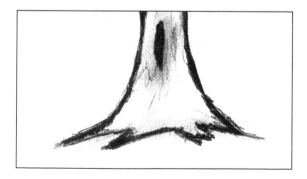

Figure 172

This style of flattened root forms a ground line in both figure 172 and figure 173 yet also acknowledges the root system. The artist of each is coming to grips with his unconscious instincts and sexual nature.

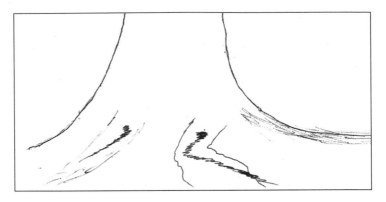

Figure 173

Notice how wide the base of the tree becomes in both figure 173 and figure 174. This indicates an openness to the unconscious nature and sexual drive. It should not surprise you to learn that all three of these figures are drawn by boys still in their early teens. The drawer of figure 173 shows convoluted roots with some odd shading. I inquired and was told he is quiet and quite mature for his age. He also has extremely bad acne and serious problems at home.

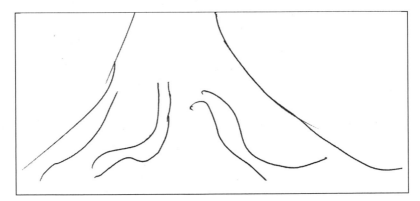

Figure 174

Look at the roots of his drawing you'll understand that the acne problem has touched even his unconscious response. The two black dots on the roots almost appear to be oozing and there is heavy shading on the masculine side, showing his doubts about himself.

Figure 174 demonstrates well-developed and defined roots. What do we know about the artist? He is a charming ninth grader, good looking, considerate, kind and a "ladies man." The girls flock around him and if he is not already sexually active, he will be soon. He shows he is on his way to a confident sexual attitude.

Girls and many boys are not aggressive in drawing the root system, in fact most eliminate roots entirely. Some have only a hint or suggestion of a root top but many keep the lower trunk connection open, or filter it through a grassy line. In figure 175 you see a normal ground line with tufts of grass, not even filtering the open trunk.

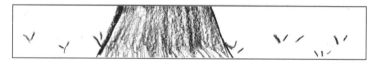

Figure 175

But here in figure 176 you see some charming tufts and flowers at the base and the sides of the trunk, trying to coyly draw your eye away from the root system and the instinctual, sexual response of the artists. Karen Bolander refers to these little tricks as "decoys." Hers was the first reference I had seen to decoys and the more you discover, the better sense the idea makes. I have never seen them around developed roots. They appear often in adult sketches.

Figure 176

Shading or shadow

- Shading or shadow is highly unusual in the sketching of young children but will show up occasionally when an older child has major parental issues. This can mean the child interprets the parent to be a problem or that the parent creates actual physical or social incidents. It is subjective, of course.

Figure 177

In figure 177 the shading on the left side in both examples indicates the problem is with the mother (dad would be toward the right). It extends into the crown in both cases, showing some serious thought has entered into the matter. The imaginary illumination comes from the right side. Is this a plus for the dad? Probably not, simply a negative response to the mother.

- If only the trunk is shaded the reaction could be more emotional than thoughtful .
- An actual shadow of a tree occurs so seldom that we should always spend some time pondering it. The tree itself is a subconscious representation of the self and one's experience, so how deep and layered does that

make the shadow of the tree? Boogity! Something very hidden, very serious and very profound resides in the shadow. In some cases this can refer to a dark, shadow side of the self, more so with adult drawings. A reminder, do not speculate.

Figure 178

The young teen who drew figure 178 draws the large trunk wide open to the massive lower sphere at the bottom of the page. The tree is left of the middle but centered vertically with clouds directly above a dominant divided crown. The child is social, with good self-esteem, but "of two minds," open to suggestion and influenced either by the mother or the artist's own dark side. The shadow placement and the flying birds confirm this. The birds are meant to be crows, "ka ka" (caw caw), which are considered unfortunate omens. They hover over the mother side and the shadow.

The anthropomorphic sun is decidedly a puzzled male image, and shows the artist's need for parental love. The ominous mask-like knothole may register an emotional masquerade of some sort in the drawer's life.

The dark spot to the left of the trunk appears to be fallen fruit, even though no other fruit is visible. It is related in some way to the shadow, representing a disappointment or a failure.

All we know is that the artist a ninth grader.

Bark
- Bark on a tree is usually just stroked-in color. When it is drawn on it serves as protection for the emotions.

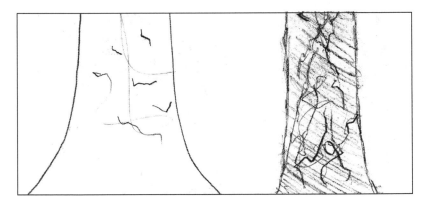

Figure 179

The difference between the needs of the two drawers in figure 179 is obvious. The one on the left has only a few squiggles while the tree on the right is very protected.

Branches

- Branches added below the crown usually relate to past experiences. In general if the branch is healthy and alive the experience was pleasant; if dead, broken or angled downward, it was unpleasant or disappointing. Examine the location for clues regarding the mother or father.

Figure 180

The trees in figure 180 were drawn by the same girl, the one on the left at about age 10, and the one on the right at age 15. You can see that the unpleasant experience from the earlier drawing has faded into what is now only a scar.

She was not aware of this, of course, but her grandmother feels she began adding the damaged branch to her tree drawings after her mother had to be rushed to the hospital, during a home delivery, for the cesarean birth of a new sibling.

Examine also the two crowns of her trees. The "squashed" look of the crown on the left has gradually rounded and begun to stretch upward in the later sketch.

Being one of the older children in a large family she often had to care for the younger ones, and did so quite willingly. She was, however, also feeling some pressure from above to help, which in this case is from the parents or an older sibling. (This trait is visible in handwriting in much the same way.) The pressure from above results in the widening of the crown, which you will see defined as a "reaching out" to others. It is, certainly, but the reasons vary from one subject to another.

- Because the branch is added to the trunk, understand that the experience can be either an actual occurrence or a reaction to emotion. Hurt feelings register in the same manner as physical trauma.
- Be aware also that children who draw together copy ideas, and the new branch (or anything else) you are seeing on your child's tree could actually be "plagiarized." Be cautious then, before you commit to the source of any tree-branch trauma.

Scars And Knotholes
- Scars or cuts represent a trauma to the drawer, usually of a lesser degree than a damaged branch. Which of us gets through childhood without some sort of trauma? Exact importance of each incident depends sometimes on how one views it.
- Knotholes and holes in the trunk are generally related to concern regarding sexual reproduction in various ways that we'll explore.

  It seems to me that younger children may take a look at the tall expanse of trunk they have created and simply feel that it looks empty. Adding the hole in the trunk fills the blank space and creates interest. Other analysts have stated that the addition of the knothole enriches the emotional sphere of the trunk. The hole in the trunk becomes the "doorway" into the tree for young children and into their spiritual interior. I can agree with all this.
- When the hole in the trunk is shelter for small animals or birds, there is interest in—or even preoccupation with—the reproductive process. You surely remember how much there was to learn about all of this!

- Adolescents, girls especially, often include knotholes in their trunks which can refer to preoccupation with the reproductive functions, including menstruation. When the knothole is darkened, some say it refers to their first experience with sexual intercourse, but I seriously doubt it. Tracking the accuracy of this seems a little dicey, but you may have a network of teens willing to provide some otherwise elusive information.

Figure 181

The two girls who drew figure 181 provide us some nice signals. Both have an interest in the instinctual, sexual sphere shown by the flare of the base of the trunk.

On the left the 7 or 8 year-old shows us that she has protected herself emotionally with some bark, is at the age when mom is dominant for her (larger, heavier branches), and has practically bisected the tree with her reproductively curious knothole. The flowing river is a nod to the feminine nature with which she identifies. She defines the trunk of her winter tree by the faint horizontal line at the crown, otherwise it would be connected only by branches.

The 14 year-old on the right is in her "daddy" phase. The small knothole shows her interest in reproduction. The bark on the trunk resembles a coiled spring. The limb represents her dominant feelings for her dad reinforcing the area well before disappearing into the crown. The bird nest suggests home is where her dad is, and the flowering crown of the tree reflects pure joy. We see an excited emerging female. Dad will be stunned when this phase passes in the blink of an eye, and he becomes a nerd overnight.

Flowers And Fruit
- Flowers and buds on a foliated tree are an anticipation of positive things, general happiness and joy.
- On a branch or a crown with no leaves there will be a subtle reason for including flowers, which will pertain to the personal needs of the artist. See figures 141 & 228.
- Fruit on a tree is a positive sign. With children, fruit can relate to projects of interest to them, or feelings of general abundance. We already know that fruit is a convenient way to subconsciously record numbers.
- Fruit that has dropped from the tree usually indicates a disappointment or a failed project. It can occasionally indicate a previous accomplishment which no longer matters to the drawer.
- Berry clusters or grapes hanging from a branch on a tree show the subject needs to have praise or validation.

Leaves
- Leaves can take many forms on and off the tree. I find very few drawings by children with individual leaves (other than palm fronds). Children seem to draw foliage for the most part rather than actual leaves. My own prejudice dictates, from information and analysis, that those who *do* draw individual leaves are among the most creative and mature of their age group. This in no way says that those who *omit* leaves are not mature or creative. One common definition of an abundance of individual leaves is dependency.
- We have discussed the use of leaves as a filter, such as in figure 144, and the use of one leaf at the end of the willow branches in figure 151 as positive anticipation.

- When one single leaf is drawn at the ends of upward-angled pointed branches it will tend to soften the relationship to the environment, and the drawer will have a positive attitude in general.
- Falling leaves show an acceptance of circumstances and the ability to handle disappointment.
- A leaf or a cluster of leaves at the end of a branch can also indicate an openly curious nature, almost probing the environment.
- A row of tight, carefully drawn leaves on both sides of a single-line branch indicates a kind of regimented thinking. Imagination is suppressed in favor of learned responses. The safe route is the presumed correct one.
- Extremely large leaves indicate active imagination, and some say, a dependent nature. A child who draws large abstract leaves demonstrates a self-confident creativity.

Figure 182

Look at how the 10 year-old girl who drew figure 182 has demonstrated this in the third tree. The large leaves in the banana tree are normal but she has closed the crown safely (protecting from influence from above) at the top, to better conform with her other closed crowns. She still has dominant trunks but the crowns are all well-developed and have a goal-oriented and upward movement. There are no branches or marks on any of the trunks to indicate distress in her life, either real or imagined.

Her pleasant picture is full of activity (high energy and enthusiasm), and the soft cloud or skyline is sketched only to fill help the page.

Look also at the amazing balance in her drawing—4 trees, 4 apples, 4 posies in the middle of the trees, 8 banana bunches—2 animals, 2 mushrooms, 2 caterpillars, 2 birds, 2 butterflies 3 sets of 2 tulips. Ah, you say, but only 1 sun (parental love, she really feels it)! Ah, say I, but the sun is balanced in counterpoint at the lower right corner by the 1 round bush!

What do we know about the child? The older of two children, she spends time after school at her parents' business doing schoolwork and drawing with her younger brother. She comes from a disciplined, loving, goal-oriented family and it shows.

The two siblings or the four nuclear family members seem to be reflected over and over in her work. The four apples in the first tree seem to be safely enclosed in pairs of arms, don't they? We see a contented child.

Small animals
• Small animals on the tree bring added energy to the part of the tree on which they appear.
• A small animal hanging from a limb by a tail or arm is a form of gentle teasing or mockery of the artist himself.
• Animals in a hole in the trunk show general concern by the artist regarding child bearing. Whether this is reluctance or positive interest has to be determined by age and other known facts.

Birds, Birdhouses And Nests
• Carefully sketched birds in the tree or flying around the tree are always harbingers of positive cheerfulness.
• Perched on the branch, the bird gives hope that all will be well.

- A bird sitting on a damaged branch, reinforces that the result of the original trauma will prove to be positive.
- The bird flying toward the tree shows a receptivity on the part of the drawer to new ideas.
- A bird flying away from the tree indicates the artist's own active ideas.
- A bird can represent a specific person to the artist.
- A nest adds energy to the portion of the tree in which it is located, especially with a bird or eggs in it.
- When located in the crotch of two branches or a trunk and a branch it expresses hope regarding the family.
- A birdhouse is a specifically crafted item and as such has a different meaning. Attached to the tree in any way, it shows a willingness to help others.

Figure 183

The 10 year-old (count the fruit) drawer of figure 183 drew three branches indicating trauma, most likely the divorce and remarriage of her parents. She lives with mom and a new stepfather. Let's look at the symbolism of the animals and birds on her dead branches, and taking the facts into consideration, view the situation as she sees it.

She and her mother are represented together as squirrels on the female side of the trunk. The lower right branch, contains the nesting bird representing dad, the new wife and their children. On the upper right side she draws the stepfather as a woodpecker, tapping on her emotional trunk, but also trying to invade the trunk where they live. Both the bird and the woodpecker are shown on the male side of the tree, and at appropriate time frames.

She admitted in later years her fear of losing her mother to a new stepfather. Examine the branch of the woodpecker, considered a prophetic and magical bird. It is reinforced and appears to be two distinct branches. It is as though she sees this as a double trauma or threat.

Fences Or Ladders

• A ladder propped against the trunk means the artist feels that other people are playing to his emotions, or trying to use his emotions for their own needs.

Figure 184

The boy who drew figure 184 was approximately 10 years-old and was literally caught in the act of trying to change his own emotions, and alter his future. Let me explain this fascinating drawing and the situation.

The facts first...his mother had divorced his dad and remarried. The boy was close to his own father before the separation and disliked the stepfather. They lived a great distance from the father. The boy begged his father to ask for custody of him from the mother, and the dad agreed. She insisted that the child stay with her and the other siblings.

Whether this drawing was made before, during or shortly after the incident, it was at the approximate time and the meaning remains the same.

The ladder against the tree trunk involves his torn emotions. Both branches on the mother side are foliated, not damaged. The trunk begins to angle toward the right, the future and the father, at the point where the stick figure starts the action (the boy asks to leave). He identifies with his father mentally, as the entire crown shifts to the right.

Still, he has these pesky positive feelings regarding his mother. The dominant branch grows from a position where the left side of the crown should originate (she is important), but angles steeply downward (she has failed him or certainly disappointed him).

He positions himself quite precariously on the lower branch (still representing the mother), much too far away to do the big job of cutting off the branch, although the scar shows he's tried. It's not an easy thing to cut one's mother out of one's life, so he has tried to enlist her help. She will make the decision whether or not to let him leave.

- Ladders forming steps made from separate pieces of wood and attached to the tree show the artist's desire to rise above the emotional field, and live in the mental or inspirational aspect of the mind. This expression will often lead to a platform, a tree house or something else in the crown of the tree.
- Fences at the base of or surrounding the tree are a form of defense, often taking the place of heavy bark. These individuals are fearful of being approached, because they feel they have no natural internal defenses.

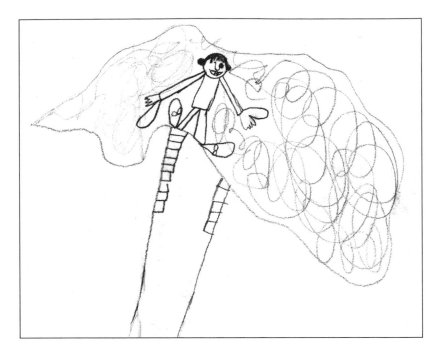

Figure 185 (132)

We revisit as promised, the little fellow from the previous chapter here in figure 185. We can now concentrate on other aspects of his male dominated tree. You notice, of course, that the whole tree tips into the masculine area of the page, and the crown itself is fully developed on the masculine side. Do you recognize the flattened crown that shows he is feeling a great deal of pressure?

You'll notice the 10 steps on the left side correspond to his age. His steps (showing the desire to rise above the emotional nature) lead only to himself, comfortably settled into the mental sphere of the crown.

This youngster had to take medication for allergies which could have affected thought patterns, but he was also known as a daydreamer (his crown is closed and has the swirls of the self-concerned). This affected his schoolwork and created pressure from parents and teachers, indicated by the compressed crown of his tree. As he matured he developed a passion for philosophy.

The Christmas Tree

Let's deal with the Christmas tree here, because it is in its own category, somewhat like a fantasy tree. It is common to find them drawn around the holiday period, but not at other times. Should a child draw a Christmas tree in another season, she may be feeling dependent and looking for love and approval. Anger can also play a part.

Figure 186

The girl who drew the tree in figure 186 included it in a series of nicely drawn trees identified by genus. This one was labeled "pine." There is one gift (for her?) placed under the branches reaching toward the father side of the page.

She had lived with her mother from an early age after her parents divorced. She had not seen him often, nor did he always remember her on birthdays nor on the holidays. Do you see the symbolism of the distorted branches done by an exceptionally good artist?

The following Christmas tree, figure 187, was drawn by a little girl with an intact family, during the holiday season.

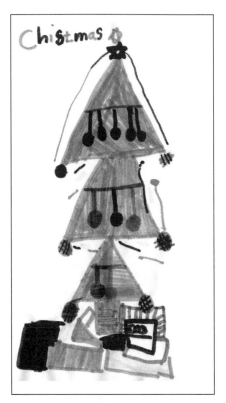

Figure 187

Direction Of The Paper

We discussed in Chapter One and again regarding figure 101 the meaning of using either the vertical or the horizontal axis of the paper for the drawing. With a tree drawing, it is important if the drawer chooses to turn the paper to the wide axis to draw the tree, giving herself more horizontal space.

Drawing on the wide axis of the page can indicate dissatisfaction with one's environment, a need for change or perhaps a tendency to escape into fantasy. This is especially true if the artist is young.

There is the feeling that the world owes the drawer something—that they deserve more than they have—just as they need more space in which to draw their tree. This explanation does not apply if the tree is part of a scene, only when the tree is drawn alone.

The drawing in figure 186 was done on the wide horizontal axis; figure 187 on the vertical axis. Both slightly left of center, with space on either side of the tree.

An Exceptional Tree

Figure 188

The 13 year-old girl responsible for figure 188 had been troubled for most of her young life by marked emotional mood swings.

When she was "up" she was charming, helpful, and a true sweetheart of a girl. When her emotions were "down" she was unrecognizable as the same child. This distressing change could happen mid-sentence while one was talking with her. As she matured, she received treatment for bipolar disorder, to the relief of the many who loved her.

Her tree appears to be a well-drawn winter tree, doesn't it? Look carefully. What is conveyed on the page is actually a drawing of two single-line fantasy trees. Nowhere do they touch or converge. Her tree sketch is an absolute echo of her condition.

Artwork and handwriting both originate in the brain. The signals created are transferred to the paper in a pure, unaltered fashion. We have only to read them.

Now I'll step off the box, refer you to the reading list in the bibliography to learn more, and define some additional symbols you'll likely find in a child's drawing.

Chapter Seven
Lines, Shapes and Alphabet Soup

*"All art is at once surface and symbol.
Those who go beneath the surface
do so at their own risk."*
<u>The Picture Of Dorian Gray</u>
Oscar Wilde

We have explored many of the most basic symbols that children use in drawings. This section provides general definitions of additional items.

As you identify certain forms in the drawing their meanings may be applied in a variety of ways. In fact a thing can have more than one meaning, so you will be forced to think everything through carefully. According to what else you see in the sketch, a definition may hold great weight or very little. Don't be rigid.

First we'll examine various lines and shapes, which we can consider to be the bones of a drawing in many cases. Then we'll flesh it all out with alphabetized definitions of common things that the child may have included in the drawing. It is left to the analyst to responsibly tweak the body of the analysis into a whole and recognizable shape.

"Tweak" has more than one meaning, of course, but as we use it here, consider it a minimal change applied to an object or idea in order to improve or make sense of it.

We are amused by the expression—attributed to both Oscar Wilde and George Bernard Shaw, and quoted by Winston Churchill—that Great Britain and America are two countries separated by a common language. There is one word, however, the Brits use freely that you could come to appreciate, and the word is "twig."

Although it is used to mean "a small branch" on both sides of the Atlantic, the English use it often as an "aha" or an understanding or appreciation of an idea or a thing, as in "I twigged to it straight away." Two young men from our immediate family have returned from extended stays in England, freely using this practical expression.

Tweak your analysis carefully, until you twig to it.

Line Direction and Quality

The way lines are constructed throughout the sketch should be more or less uniform. Notice any lines that are reinforced or erased. We want any correction to bring an improvement to the drawing. Lines are read by pressure and stroke direction, as we learned in Chapter One.

Crosshatching over another object Shows anxiety, usually regarding the object covered over.

Dark border around a drawing Is an emphasis on the sketch, of course. Try to understand why, and be sure it wasn't done as an afterthought in a daydreaming state.

Dark, heavy lines Call strong attention to themselves and the object, or part of the object, being drawn.

Dashes or broken lines Show a concern for self, not in an egocentric way, but regarding one's wellbeing or health. In an extreme instance could indicated a deterioration of ego.

Faint lines Display a lack of energy, perhaps insecurity and in some cases an indicator of depression.

Fragmentation or fading of lines Analysts say this *could* indicate a neurological problem. There is, at the very least, a dissipation of energy.

Heavy line moving left This may be considered "heading backwards" in the western cultures who write and draw from left to right. Some say it is a symptom of introversion. Use caution, as this could be only reminiscing.

Jabbing marks on the paper May demonstrate anger and/or petulance. At what or whom? Maybe at oneself.

Jagged lines High energy and usually a sign of anger or frustration. Where are they? Inside another form indicates an attempt to contain anger. Located outside another form could indicate something as serious as a desire for revenge.

Straight, solid lines Certainly indicate determination and decisiveness. They may display aggression, especially when not used routinely in the child's drawing.

Ticked, jerky lines Display impatience or anxiety in the form of nervousness.

Unusually neat, orderly lines Show a need for a structured environment. These lines differ, of course, from the obvious ruler-drawn lines.

Upward lines and points Are drawn by high achievers. The more pointed and probing they are, the more intellectually penetrating the mind of the artist.

Common Shapes and Forms

Arrow By their nature they draw your attention to the direction which they point, so pay attention and decipher them according to figure 8. Arrows can often indicate a sense of harm, so notice whether they point at someone. If the artist is identifying figures with names there is no harm intended. Some say they signify ambition. This can be so, if they point upward or toward the right. Always ask yourself what is in the path of the arrow (s).

Boxes Are drawn by self-contained, yet receptive people who are, or want to be, organized in their thinking and/or surroundings. Those children who draws three-dimensional boxes enjoy solving problems. A box drawn inside another box is an indicator of frustration. The box is considered a feminine (enclosing) form.

Circle As we covered in Chapter Five, a very feminine, and absolutely social symbol. The circle is the beginning and the end...completion and wholeness.

Cone A symbol of fertility and fruitfulness, considered both a phallic and a feminine symbol. It holds aspects of creativity and good fortune.

Cross Used almost exclusively as a religious symbol. Several crosses drawn together seem to offer the artist a sense of protection.

Diamond This four-sided geometric shape has its points probing in all directions. Those who draw diamonds have a penetrating intellectual curiosity. They can demonstrate both superficiality and thoroughness. A symbol of sincerity, incorruptibility and femininity.

Dot A most overlooked and often ignored symbol. One dot alone is the signal of the self. The artist will emphasize it, usually by circling over and over. When you find one, consider it the focal point of the drawing, then see how other signals relate to it. The drawn dot will stand by itself rather than be incorporated into another symbol, such as a pupil of an eye or a navel.

Many dots Show a sense of unease or indicate some form of intimidation. If a child has dotting around a shape it indicates he is having trouble understanding what it means, or he is trying to puzzle through some aspect of a person or a situation.

Heart Drawn by those—most often young girls, in fact almost all young girls—who feel compassion and love. Drawing hearts within other hearts shows a strong desire to express your affection. The heart symbol is used routinely by girls of all ages. It will be found incorporated into drawings or drawn in groups, with or without arrows and elaborate designs. Through the ages the heart has been recognized as the center of being, love and truth. When a heart is linked with another, even though meant as a love link, the artist shows a capacity for empathy. The heart pierced by an arrow may demonstrate the "pain of love" or regret. Notice if the arrow points at a specific thing, person or name.

Loops Are deceptive because they appear so casual and lazy, but they are always seeking excitement. The artists who use loops are imaginative and energetic types. The littler folks who draw loops commonly behave in a charming, if not openly flirtatious, fashion. Wide, full loops are an almost expression of boredom, while those tight, narrow loops touching each other are becoming "uptight" and had better find something interesting to do. "She's a little loopy" can be a very accurate description. Tightly swirled loops may betray a tendency to worry, especially when used overhead in a drawing.

Mosaic These drawings are done by those with rational, orderly minds. While fitting geometric forms together can be seen as obsessive, it is actually a calming activity.

Oval A feminine representation of life. In many cultures the oval is synonymous with innocence. It will often show up in the form of a halo in a child's drawing.

Pyramid An accepted symbol for the female breast in therapy, but more important, the seat of the creative power of the sun, therefore, the center of the universe. A powerful, magical, masculine symbol in Egyptian and Aztec cultures. Always a signal of creativity.

Rainbow The child who draws a rainbow is conveying a sense of transformation, which is to say, she may be "pulling herself up by her bootstraps." She may get into a little funk but is confident that things will get better. A great trait in a child. This shows confidence and faith in her life. A rainbow offers protection to anything drawn under it.

Spiral These guys can be wonderful when expanding outward, but wretched when closing tightly into the center. It all has to do with the direction of the energy, as the spiral has always represented a dynamic life force. We'll discuss a bit more in the next chapter. You can see by the stroke and pressure the direction from which a spiral is formed.

Square Represents the earthly forms. Combined with the circle in a mandala, it is symbolic of the union of heaven with earth. Those who draw squares are honest, grounded and straightforward people. They may also be more aggressive (especially when called...).

Teardrop A completely feminine form, like the oval we have seen before in Chapter Five. There is, in this form, a suggestion of sadness, so keep an eye on the artist.

Tornado When those loops pile on each other and pick up speed, you have a symbol exploding with emotional turmoil. Where is it headed and how to divert it?

Trapezoid This irregular form commands your attention as all awkward forms do. This six-sided shape signals that some aspect of the artist or his life needs to change. There is often an inner struggle to be resolved.

Triangle The upward triangle signals an attitude of high achievement and percolating ambition. These folks may or may not be openly aggressive, but they are most certainly movers, shakers and doers. If the triangle points downward, an unusual position, you will find the sketcher to be more passive, while still committed.

Water and waves Water may portray the mother. It always represents the female influence. Water sketches can also be an indication of subconscious emotional conditions. If the waves are large the artist feels overwhelmed with something in his life. Some analysts say anything drawn beneath the water can signify anger or helplessness. I can't blindly agree. We see pleasant underwater scenes in children's drawings, sometimes inspired by aquariums. Consider the way the water is drawn. Water is always mystery.

Wheel Signifies progress or movement. Can indicate change of any sort in one's life or thinking patterns.

X's When included in the design of anything (clothing, doorways etc.) drawn in the sketch, casts a negative or suspicious aspect on it. Ask yourself why.

ABC's

Here are some of the more common items the child or adolescent will use to embellish or complete a drawing.

Remember, you can find the sun, house, additions to the house, the person and parts of the body in Chapter Five.

– A –

Airplane A need to escape, or to move on. This might be satisfied by a brief trip or even a daydream fantasy.

Angel Drawn by enlightened, gentle, easy-going souls. Can show a preoccupation with religion, or curiosity regarding a recent death.

Apple The sign of wisdom, peace, knowledge and fertility. It also has the flip side of deceitfulness—*à la* Adam and Eve, or the wicked queen's poisoning of Snow White.

Apron Tidiness and self-protection, even to include one's protection in the sense of sexually "covering up."

Animals Usually reflect the artist's idea of himself. Domestic animals may be drawn to show a harmless, natural occurrence. Wild animals may be utilized to convey a more dangerous or adventurous happening.

– B –

Bag Shows concealment or a secret. Something may be hidden by the artist or, he may feel, hidden from him.

Ball Carries the meaning of the circle. If a small ball in the picture is to be hit, check the trajectory it will travel.

Balloon Playfulness and a carefree attitude. Remember our discussion of the sun, and the desire to rise above a current situation. If deflated, can signal frustration.

Basket The symbol for abundance and generosity, more so when full. The end of a cycle when tipped over. A child who draws an empty basket (or similar container) feels deprived of material goods or love.

Bell Drawn by those who are respectful and obedient. Also a symbol of creative power.

Belly Button A very small or a missing navel is a sign of independence. A large one shows a defensive attitude, a need for protection, or "a desire to return to the womb."

Belt When exaggerated can indicate self-consciousness over sexual matters. A large buckle shows authority or strength, so notice who wears it.

Birds Represent ideas and ideals. Harbingers of good things. A flock of birds coming your way is a desire for friends. Flying away, it represents your capacity for fertile ideas. Flying birds demonstrate a desire for freedom. A bird may represent a certain person in the artist's life.

Boats A female symbolism often showing the need to be nourished and cuddled. A boat on peaceful water shows a

sense of security but a boat on stormy seas may indicate anxiety over a female relative (perhaps the mother?).

Book Shows a capacity to learn, especially when open.

Boots Dressy boots display an intense interest in sexual matters. Considered a sexual symbol.

Bows A signal that the artist likes and responds to flattery. The artist may appear competent and orderly.

Bottle An enclosing or containing symbol which can signal a form of inhibition.

Breasts Any obvious representation shows the artist is still dependent and has a need to be nurtured.

Bridge Indicates a strong tendency toward problem solving and connections. Even the young sketcher of bridges may have an unusual and facile ability to connect opposites.

Bull Signifies strength and dominance.

Butterfly The symbol for transformation and rebirth. Used by children as a way of making things better.

Buttons A prime demonstration of dependency, often shown as small circles, signaling sociability also. May be drawn on the person upon whom they feel dependent.

– C –

Car Represents progress and comfort.

Castle Shows a desire for luxury and status.

Cat The animal symbol for domesticity. The desire for, or the depiction of, a warm and comfortable home. Conversely, some say the presence of a cat shows a serious conflict or competition with the mother.

Chain The sign for unity but can also show constraint. If a link is broken, the artist feels constrained and has a need for some form of freedom.

Chair The symbol for relaxation and leisure. When empty, the sketcher may want some down time.

Chessboard or checkerboard Problems on the mind and a need to solve them.

Clown Demonstrates some hidden unhappiness. The artist feels a responsibility to keep others content and cheered up.

Corn On the cob or stalk, a sign of abundance.
Cow This domestic animal may signify abundance.
Collar on clothing The artist is dignified and formal or may feel a heavy sense of responsibility.
Crow Considered an omen of bad luck. Rarely drawn.
Cup Drawn by a generous person.
Curly hair Considered a flattering addition to a person, usually indicating affection and respect.

– D –

Daisy Commonly used flower representing contentment and a happy outlook.
Dog The domestic animal representing loyalty. When the dog is drawn snarling, the artist may feel betrayed.
Dollar signs Obviously, money on the mind.
Donkey A symbol of humility, but also foolishness.
Dolphin A sign of transformation.
Dragon or sea serpent A sign of good and evil. The artist is in some sort of struggle, perhaps within himself.
Drum Believed to show repressed anger.
Duck Floating in water, shows superficiality.

– E –

Eagle Indication of pride and lofty ideals.
Earrings Used as feminine adornment. Might also show a tendency to put too much stress on what is heard.
Eggs Refers to family issues when drawn in a nest, or the artist may have concerns regarding the birth process. Can also be a sign of creativity.
Elephant Symbol of strength, memory and patience.

– F –

Feather Always represents lightness and truth. In some cultures it signifies the soul.
Fence Primarily, a desire for protection, but with a gate drawn, can also indicate a strong compulsion to be free.
Fire Any symbol that generates heat is a strong longing for warmth and in some cases, nurturing and love.
Fish References peace or procreation. Religious symbol.

Flowers Some blooms have individual meanings. Consider the shape as well as the essence. They signify appreciation of beauty, but are short lived. A drawing of a bud shows room for growth. A flower or a bouquet at full bloom is in peak development. A bloom with a cup shape signifies generosity. A bouquet shows contentment and love of beauty.
Fly Associated with destruction and pestilence.
Fly swatter or whisk Power, leadership and authority.
Forest A recognized place of testing, therefore, darkness and the unknown. The artist may feel challenged on some level.
Fountain A symbol of regeneration and purity.
Freckles Usually used by the sketcher as a symbol of self-consciousness.
Frog Signifies transformation and regeneration.
Fruit Symbol of generosity, abundance and basic pleasures. Prosperity of spirit is shown by the sharing of fruit.

– G –

Garbage Occasionally drawn by children jealous of the arrival of a new sibling. Can depict competition. Some say the drawer may feel that he, himself, lacks worth.
Gate Can show a desire to protect, or to leave something behind and start over with something new.
Giraffe Considered a phallic reference. Drawn by those exploring their sexuality.
Grapes An indication of wisdom. Remember, when drawn on a bare tree branch, the artist needs praise or validation in some area of his life.
Gun Male power and authority. See where it is aimed.

– H –

Hair Always a symbol of strength and life force on the head. Sparse hair indicates a feeling of inadequacy, yet complete lack of hair on the head does not show lack of strength. (!!) Mussed hair on the head shows confusion. Body hair on a male indicates virility.
Hammer or other dangerous tool Thought by some to relate to unexpressed anger and passive-aggressive behavior.

Hat The wearer is looking for some special attention.

Horns Represent strength and power. A way of opening a path for oneself, because the area ahead is cleared.

Horse Represents speed, power, mastery. Popular with young girls, thought to be associated with sexual curiosity.

Hourglass   Awareness of time passing. Where is the sand?

– I –

Ice or icicles If out of place in a seasonal drawing, the artist may be stuck with a grudge he needs to dismiss.

Insects Are negative thoughts or irritating things the drawer must come to grips with. Preoccupations.

Ivy Demonstrates tenacity and constant friendship.

– J –

Jewelry or gems Gives added attention or energy when drawn on a figure in a picture. Can indicate ambition.

Jump rope   Can be an encapsulation or a competition.

– K –

Key A powerful indicator of choice and freedom of action. Authority to gain access to knowledge and privilege. Can be considered phallic, especially when drawn by a lock with a visible keyhole, but look beyond this. Could be considered a turning point for the artist in some way.

Kite The need or desire to escape a situation or a responsibility, usually something specific. Often a kite is associated with feelings of restriction.

Knife Yes, this can be an aggressive expression, but not always. There could be a desire to cut something out of, or away from, one's life, or to carve out a place for one's self. Perhaps the artist needs freedom from a symbolic umbilical cord or apron strings?

Knot Often drawn to show restriction. This may be a symbol of restraint or a signal of union. How is it used ?

– L –

Ladder A common symbol, thought in the past to be an indicator of ambition. More sensibly, now it registers the steps taken to gain one's current position or goals in life.

Lamp A lamp represents the need for warmth and in some cases, nurturing. It shows not only the desire to receive warmth, but also the ability to give and share it.

Light bulb Knowledge and illumination. Logically, a common symbol of "an idea." All lights show warmth.

Lightning All angled shapes and lines show dynamic energy. Lightning can be used to indicate the power in either fear or enlightenment.

Lion Kids use the powerful lion in "the king of the beasts" sense to evoke majesty and dominance.

Lock It may be used as a barrier for the artist or maybe he's in the process of opening doors for himself.

Logs or woodpiles Masculinity in its hyper condition, as in the breast-beating competitive state.

Lizard A silent creature. Can be used to hide a secret.

– M –

Mask The sketcher may be very private or not like to have people know his true feelings. In extreme cases the artist may be concealing his personality or life. It is also a way of saying "don't look at this, look beyond."

Maze Has two different interpretations. The artist can be confused and frustrated, or can be very adept at working through to successful conclusions. Look for either a solid pathway or futile dead ends in the maze.

Mirror Can show vanity or enlightenment. How is it used and how is the reflection displayed? A mirror can also be interpreted as a search for truth.

Monkey An energetic and curious nature. Hanging by an arm, it shows a tendency to make fun of one's self.

Monster Life may contain insurmountable problems for the artist. Drawing monsters makes them seem manageable.

Moon The hidden, intuitive side of nature. The artist may be preoccupied with the natural cycles and occurrences in life and nature. Feminine symbol.

Mountains Represent goals and ideals. Those who enjoy a challenge often draw mountains.

Mouse A sign of timidity, or perhaps unnecessary fear or turbulence in the drawer's life.

Muscles Commonly drawn by young boys. The overly muscled figure signals either a state of self-absorption or insecurity, usually regarding the artist's own manliness.

Music Notes and treble clefs are drawn in an attempt to bring joy or lightheartedness into a drawing.

Mustache Commonly drawn to show virility or mockery.

– N –

Name Drawing names of others (or one's own name) is a common adolescent pastime and signals that the person is on the artist's mind. How the name is embellished will provide clues to the emotion involved.

Nest Usually drawn in a tree and represents the need to be nurtured. With eggs, consider it a desire for family.

Net Shows power over another. How is it used?

– O –

Owl Signifies wisdom and magical powers.

– PQ –

Pairs When things are drawn in sets of two it always signals a sense of opposites or dualities.

Pants Competence and authority, but only if they fit. If too big, small, short, long or baggy they convey "nerdiness."

Parrot Link between human and spirit worlds.

Peacock Regal pride. Thought to be incorruptible.

Pear The symbol of mother or love or both.

Pebbles or stones Especially on a pathway, signify obstacles to be overcome.

Pig A sign of courage in some cultures, but children often use it to represent selfishness and even filth.

Pineapple Represents sociability and fertility.

Pockets Determine what they are used for in the sketch. Are the pockets used to hide the hands? Pockets at hipline on a girl are feminine. Shirt pockets on a male are considered gender confusion by some analysts.

Profiles May be considered evasive, when routinely drawn.

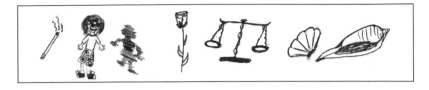

Purse Used for containment and conservation of important items. Pertains to responsibilities of life and health.

– R –

Rabbit Speed and fertility. Considered good luck.

Rain Should be considered cleansing, but is often tied to depression. How does it feel in the drawing?

Rat Commonly used in fear as a symbol for pestilence, filth and death. Positives? Yes, cleverness and tenacity.

Rocks Show strength and a stability of character. They are seen as major obstacles though, if placed on a pathway.

Rose The most developed blossom. Purity, perfection and all of life's mystery. Used as a religious symbol. The thorns represent sin and the pain of loving.

– S –

Scales Represent judgement. The child who draws a set of scales is likely to think before acting.

Scroll Shows traditional law or absolute authority.

Seashells Appreciation of love and beauty. Can also be a demonstration of needing protection or desire to hide.

Shadow Personal shadow shows a different side of the self, usually believed to be well-hidden. May also reflect creative impulses not acted upon. Not always ominous.

Shoes Provide a portion of our foundation. Small feet and shoes may show humility, or when shaded, insecurity. Large or elongated, the child may feel unstable and in need of grounding. Can be a phallic symbol, especially when the foot is included. Very high stiletto heels are sending an openly sexual message.

Skirt Represents feminine identification. A long skirt may show inhibition. The short one shows the artist has nothing to hide and perhaps is flirtatious. When highly decorated can show concern, often in a compulsive way, regarding the artist's idea of femininity. Interpret the designs on the skirt.

Smoking Whether cigarette, cigar or pipe it indicates a preoccupation with adult behavior. Phallic symbol.

Snail May represent concern with birth process. Contains both male and female symbolism.

Snakes Many interpretations. Obvious phallic reference of sexual tension. Unpredictability and temptation may be present also. Fertility, spirituality and healing are embodied in snakes. And don't ignore the yuck factor for boys!

Spider Considered more ominous than other insects, especially with a web included which signals a trap. Conversely, it can be a metaphor for clever, intricate capacity to build. It will relate entirely to its use in the drawing.

Stairway Holds much of the symbolism of the ladder, but carries the meaning a step (pun intended) further. Going upward gains enlightenment while heading down a stairway propels one into darkness. A spiral set of stairs represents mystery and the unknown. A simple set of steps shows how receptive the individual is socially. Zigzag steps seen from the side going nowhere signals a dead end, or energy expended for nothing.

Stars Indicate the desire for wish fulfillment. Some say they signify unrealized ambition. And yet another interpretation is emotional or physical depravation.

Stripes Show concerns or problems with something in one's everyday life. When they are drawn on clothing there may be negativity regarding that specific part of the body.

Swan Conveys serenity and peace. The swan seems private and apart from other species. Those who draw them may feel they, themselves, are special and a notch "above."

Sword Symbol of power, courage and authority. Heroes from all cultures wield a noble sword. In myth and fable the sword is commonly used to divide good from evil.

– T –

Table A social symbol. Many pleasant things happen at a table. The number of chairs included may be relevant.

Teepee See the reference to the triangle. The teepee shape can indicate stubbornness in certain situations.

Tongue A visible tongue in a child's drawing is disturbing when not used for a specific facial gesture. See the further explanation in Chapter Eight.

Tower A symbol of authority in a scene. A figure in the tower may be isolated, or may feel superior to peers.

Toys Drawn in abundance or prominently show that the artist often has to deal with temptation.

Truck Shows a desire for progress and power.

Tulip The cup shape indicates generosity. The tulip is an expressive flower of eloquence, gentility and honesty.

Tunnel Heading into the darkness of a hole, or a cave, can signal a foreboding, dread or even depression.

Turtle or tortoise Indicator of longevity, but may be a signal of shyness or even introversion. A surprising number of children draw turtles. Include and consider the meaning of the mosaic pattern of the shell in the interpretation.

– U –

Umbrella A flirtatious feminine signal if self is drawn beneath it, especially without rain, but always a sign that the child wants sheltering or protection.

Underwear Reflects either a self-consciousness, a possible vulnerability, or a preoccupation with sexual matters.

Unicorn An asexual venture into fantasy. Can reflect a wishful state of purity. A mythical animal full of gentleness and good will, which may indicate the artist is also.

– V –

Vase As with all containers, a feminine expression of abundance, safety and receptivity to all good things.

Vegetables Show a healthy attitude regarding life in general, and a need for nourishment and growth.

Vines Tangled vines show confusion, even frustration. Well-drawn, trailing vines show a need for constancy in life and security. The artist will be a faithful friend.

Violet Yes, the symbol of modesty. Those who draw violets will never toot their own horns.

Volcano Always a signal of anger. If the volcano is active or smoking, the child's anger may be obvious.

Vulture While it is seen as a symbol of destruction and exploitation, it is also a powerful symbol of protection.

– W –

Walls Represent transition and protection. Tall walls show a tendency toward fantasy. See Chapter Five.

Walnut As all nuts, they represent hidden wisdom and strength. The walnut can also symbolize selfishness, probably because nothing grows beneath a walnut tree.

Wand or baton Is endowed with magical power.

Weaving This complexity is drawn by patient and rather controlling folks who tend to accumulate things, including knowledge. They enjoy being consulted by others and will share their knowledge.

Well A feminine representation which may be the womb itself, to the artist. Abundance and mystery.

Windmill Represents balance and the ability to flow with the currents and circumstances.

Wind Vital breath of the universe, hence, life itself. Is the artist walking with it or against it?

Whip Signifies authority, domination or punishment.

Wings A prime symbol of freedom and movement. They are also drawn to depict protection.

Wolf Ferocity, guile and cruelty. Or it can signify loyalty, courage and nourishing nature. How is it pictured?

Woodpecker A magical and prophetic bird, guardian of both trees and kings.

Worm Associated with the earth, desolation, and sometimes death. Physicians, as well as therapists, say to consider the presence of pinworms, not unusual in youngsters.

Wreath A sign of glory or victory, even holiness, when placed on or around a venerated object or person.

– XYZ –

Zebra A "horse" that can't be tamed. The artist likes being perceived as unusual, perhaps even wild.

These definitions will not stay with you completely, so refer to them often. And always consider the opposite or converse meaning of the symbol. There is a tendency to get stuck on one meaning for one symbol.

Consider the geographic area in which a child lives, if the mountains or the seas predominate in their drawings. We don't see a lot of ocean waves and seashells in sketches, here in Colorado. And children in Nebraska and Montana will tend, naturally, to have great expanses of clouds and skyline in their drawings.

If you are completely puzzled by a drawing, ask the child to explain what certain aspects of it mean to him. What a concept, hmm? Ask how he feels when he draws a particular feature. Or ask if anyone has told him a story regarding his drawing or something in it.

Here is a example of a drawing we know nothing about, and never will. A teacher handed it to me in a group of accumulated pictures and said "what does this mean?" Well, who could know? She had taught first grade. We know it is right side up by the pencil strokes. We don't have a name. The sun with a 12 in it is under what looks like a crustacean leg comprised of 11 segments. A child of someone in the "12 step program" of AA? It remains a mystery.

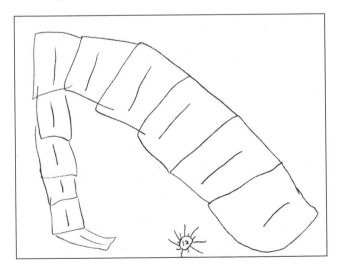

Figure 189

Chapter Eight
Trauma, Trouble And Tension

"There is only one time when it is essential to awaken…
that time is now."
Buddha

Do not read this chapter casually. Do not assume you know all you need to when you've finished it. Do not scan a drawing looking for the signals you'll be exposed to here. Most people will never be exposed to these signals in a child's drawing. Be thankful.

This chapter is included only because the abuse of a child shocks us almost senseless, yet there is case after case showing up in the news, and countless others go unreported. Many of us know personally of circumstances that never become public. If a teacher or a grandparent can be alerted— by solid signals from a child's hand—to intervene in a bad situation, this chapter will have served a purpose.

A bit of wisdom attributed to Sigmund Freud found its way into my files. Though it is quoted without an original source, the message has great value…"he who has eyes to see and ears to hear may convince himself that no mortal can keep a secret. If his lips are silent, he chatters with his fingertips; betrayal oozes out of him at every pore."

So it is with many children who have been taken advantage of by adults. They find themselves in the further disadvantaged situation of protecting the abuser, often because the child blames himself or herself, or is ashamed or afraid to seek help. But the horrendous pressure will find a way out, often on paper.

Art therapists work with these children, many of whom are quite young and unable to communicate. Across the country countless children take refuge with a mother in a women's shelter. These therapists deserve great credit. I could not find the necessary courage to endure the onslaught of unhappiness.

Some art therapists have compiled drawings by abused children. You will find some references in the bibliography for further scrutiny. The symbols children use are so universal, they can almost be considered a language, or something like the shorthand information signals used by men in hobo camps during the great depression era.

The symbols you will learn to recognize cannot be considered the only ones, nor can the use of *one or more* of these symbols be considered absolute proof of abuse, sexual or otherwise.

A child in trouble or trauma will exhibit other signs of stress. Withdrawal from others is one of the primary signs, usually accompanied by a problem with school and grades that plummet. Don't leap to any sort of conclusion regarding signals in the drawing unless there is a personality change or obvious social problems. Even then, the stresses on our youth are numerous and varied, and many, if not most, are related to peer issues. You cannot be too cautious.

In this section there will be no personalization of the sketches, only a generalization of those traits that alert therapists, psychiatrists or psychologists that they *might be, could be, perhaps are,* looking at some form of abuse.

Any form of abuse can devastate an individual.

Scattering Of Body Parts Or Disorganization

Figure 190

Scattering of body parts, such as in figure 190, where nothing is anchored to anything else on the body, shows a mind in disarray. In this example, which is not as dramatic as some, there is also a partial encapsulation.

Disorganization of the body is often seen at the shoulder line. This, as we know, is the location of power in the body. Would you say a child who could draw figure 191 might have a female power person around who is verbally abusive? The stressed mouth and fingers alert us too.

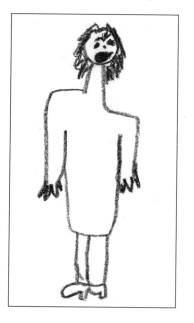

Figure 191

In some examples cataloged in the works of art therapists, children have had such miserable experiences that the body they draw is not recognizable as human.

Children of any age who have been abused may demonstrate a regression in their artwork, part of the time or all of the time. If you should notice this happening and the child herself seems troubled or withdrawn, you should contact a professional and get some help.

Children who have been abused run the gamut of emotion and behavior, and one may not react like another.

Self Deprecation

A consistent tendency for the child to draw himself in a self-deprecating manner is troublesome. An abused child will depict himself this way because of shame and low self-esteem, whether the abuse is verbal or physical.

Deprecation is defined as a loss of value, and that is what has happened to a child in this situation. They see themselves as worthless, used, devalued and in many cases, as unclean.

The example we see in figure 192 shows this in a major way. Other signals in this picture include the hands behind the back, the long, vulnerable neck, the shaded pants and the heavy stress on the belt at the waist.

Figure 192

In figure 193 there are three separate indicators. The most obvious is that of self-deprecation. Another is the heart shape of her blouse. Finally, the image is stopped at or above the waist. We'll consider these two shortly.

Is the short prickly hair, visible under the curls in this transparency, saying that there is something hidden, as there would be under a wig? Or, that the outward view is pretty but beneath it lies something else? We don't know.

Figure 193

Empty Eyes, Tears And Makeup

These signals will not necessarily appear together in a drawing, but any one of them can be a trigger for you to further examine the message of the drawing, or ask to see others drawn by the child.

Tears have an obvious meaning. But they can show up in any drawing as an expression of sadness.

Empty eyes are normal in a young child's effort. Very young children are lucky to get any semblance of an eye in the right location. At some point, however, the child adds a pupil to the eye, and usually always thereafter.

Therapists comment on the vacant look in the eyes of many abuse victims, and pay attention when they show up in a drawing. It may represent an unwillingness of the victim to acknowledge what has happened. It is not known.

Figure 194

Here in figure 194 we have empty eyes, tears and a full encapsulation of a head without a body. There can be other reasons for this drawing, such as feeling self pity for shallow reasons, but if the child's behavior has changed, investigate further with a professional.

Girls in general, and especially older victims of abuse, will draw their females in full, heavy makeup and often in glamorous outfits. Please, don't leap to any sort of distressed conclusion if your granddaughter presents you with a glamour shot! This is an outright feminine trait, but it is one that girls who have been abused tend to routinely use. Look further in the drawing.

Figure 195

The drawing above looks almost ghoulish with the empty eyes. Care has been taken with all of the other facial features and the makeup, but the eyes are vacant. The eyes could have been interpreted as closed, had the definite addition of the top lashes not been included.

This small drawing also stops short of the body.

Head And Upper Body

Drawings of only the head are quite common in abuse cases. You see this in both the preceding drawings. The head may have a pleasant face or expression. It could even be drawn peering outward from a window.

Those drawings including a body will very often stop at the waistline such as the one in figure 193 and in the following drawing. The sketch may even suggest that the figure is standing behind a table or another piece of furniture. Other ways to accomplish the same purpose is to put the figure inside of a vehicle or a boat.

Therapists speculate that a victim chooses not to deal with the genital areas. This omission may be a coping mechanism or a child may be in a state of denial.

In figure 196 you see the body cut off before reaching the waistline and full, heavy makeup on the eyelashes and mouth. We have to wonder about the "X's" on the clothing (a sign of negativity or protection).

Figure 196

The Tongue

A tongue extended out of the mouth or visible in the mouth is yet another signal that alerts therapists to the possibility of abuse. Do examine the intent, however.

Figure 197

Both of these drawings in figure 197 seem to accommodate the presence of the extended tongue as though it is a natural expression. There is no confusion about how to place the teeth and the lips.

Perhaps you remember the tongue in figure 49 in Chapter Two. This is an entirely different expression, as would be a drawing of an obstinate brat with crinkled eyes, a crinkled nose and a tongue sticking out.

Out of curiosity, I asked a 9 year-old girl to draw a picture of a face with the tongue sticking out for me. I wanted to see how easy it would be for her to do it, as well as how it would look. You see the result below in figure 198. Even after all the erasures she wasn't comfortable with it.

I asked her to draw one other picture for me on the same occasion, figure 201, which we'll examine shortly.

Figure 198

Hands And Hearts

Notice the hands if they are present (or even if they are not) in a picture. You remember that missing hands show helplessness. Hands and arms behind the back *can* indicate guilt or even hostility, and an unwillingness to face a situation. Remember?

In the case of the drawing in figure 199 notice how the hands cover the genital area. Any time you see this you know there is a reluctance about, or avoidance of, this area.

This is not routinely a signal of abuse, but can indicate a lack of comfort by the drawer when considering sexual matters. The legs, drawn tightly locked together in this sketch, are perhaps a further clue.

Consider our vamp, represented back in figure 107, who had no problem with the placement of the father's hand on the mother's abdomen. The sketch below would suggest a contrasting comfort level.

Figure 199

Any form of heart is natural for a young girl to draw, as we said in the last chapter. Be clear not to confuse this issue with the following information.

A child involved in an incestuous relationship can be understandably confused regarding love. Therapists say that the use of the heart shape will show up often in the art of girls abused in this manner, especially in self-imagery. These girls may behave in a seductive and sexual way with men in general.

Figure 200

The heart shape is found on clothing or in the shape of the mouth in both subtle and obvious portrayal. There is of course, a fine line to tread in dealing with the heart shape. In this expression in figure 200, the bottom of the bodice as well as the open front of the dress point to the genital area, which is marked and highlighted with a bow.

I had an older girl draw this with precise elements from examples of known cases of 10 year-olds, yet without copying exactly. One picture, drawn by an incest victim, had a "flower" over the genital area, showing a precise and complete drawing of male genitalia.

Figure 201

Figure 201 is the other picture our 9 year-old drew on request, after she drew the tongue in figure 198. She had no picture from which to copy; only my exuberant description of a girl going to a ball and of a gorgeous dress. I gestured and explained the heart-shaped bodice, using the word "slinky." What a difference innocence makes, hmm?

The upward attitude of the arms shows the girl dancing, and she spent a lot of time on the bows and the netting of the shoes. The crescents on the hearts represent reflections on a shiny material.

Should you see heart shapes in unusual places and used strangely such as in figure 202, the circumstances could bear some investigation. Is the behavior of the child suspect? Consult with a professional.

The house is not grounded, the dark door is floating and provides no doorknob. There are abundant hearts in the flowers, the chimney smoke and the obvious windows.

Figure 202

Beware Of False Signals

I once had an acquaintance who refused to accept excuses, whether from an employee, a friend or a child. His attitude could be philosophical, sympathetic or cynical, but his answer was always the same: "you've got to be smarter than..."

"I thought the mail had gone"..."you've got to be smarter than the mail."

"I thought the box was empty"..."you've got to be smarter than the box."

"Dad, I didn't know the door was open"..."you've got to be smarter than the door."

Over the years his comeback has stayed with me. You may have even noticed that I've used it prior to now. So...prepare yourself...

...you have got to be smarter than the drawing you are trying to interpret.

A drawing such as the one in figure 203 might create a false impression, considering all of the symbolism we have covered in this section. You must know something about the artist and her circumstances before venturing an opinion. Does that sound familiar? It cannot be stressed too often. The following examples could get one into trouble.

Figure 203

Granted, the cake decoration tube is phallic, and the plate too, perhaps. Those word balloons are a phallic shape, the girls are both drawn with tongues coming out of their mouths, their "hands" clenched in front and the drawings stop at the general site of the waist. Here are many signals in one picture—but they are all innocent!

This happy little artist is portraying nothing more than a soon-to-be-here birthday party with her sister. The anticipation of the cake has her sketching them licking their lips and holding tightly to their own hands in order to resist sampling the frosting. The cake is positioned on a suggested counter or table, though it is not drawn, so the bodies are completed to the same position. Know the artist.

Let's take another look at the heart we examined in figure 131, reproduced in figure 204.

Because the apparently happy girl has exhibited no change of behavior, is a good student, and shows no sign of social withdrawal, there is absolutely no reason to be suspicious of this rather phallic drawing. It means exactly what we discussed in Chapter Five.

Figure 204 (131)

Presumption is what you must guard against. It would be easy to leap to a false conclusion, if you regard the drawing alone.

Another situation in which you must also exercise caution is that of a child's drawing of a partially or fully naked adult. As discussed in Chapter Five, this may be the last taboo in our culture, but certain children may draw themselves as "grown up," and certainly most have seen their individual parents naked. In such drawings the breasts of a woman or genitalia of a male can be quite exaggerated, so again, you have to be smarter than the drawing, to understand the meaning.

Certain of these drawings can take one by surprise, of course. Examples are not included, in order to stay "user friendly." Some adults have a low comfort level with the issue, and some others will be concerned about children inadvertently browsing through the book.

Though you will probably rarely—or never—see the preceding serious symbols, you will often run across signals in drawings that alert you to tension or concerns affecting the drawer. Let's explore some of these.

Teachers and parents can tell you that when there is a national or a community concern, children will feel it and express it in their drawings.

Their sketches will reflect natural calamities such as forest fires and earthquakes, and the newsworthy acts of heroic people, such as astronauts. This was the case after September 11, 2001 when children across our country (and doubtless, in many other countries around the world) drew expressions of their fear and grief revolving around the twin towers of the World Trade Center in New York City. Others found solace in drawing the flag, so prominently displayed.

Figure 205

The flagpole is hard to see in figure 205. In the upper left this young boy included a bright sun. Parental love and reassurance was present in his message.

Figure 206

Tension

In figure 206 you see the rigidity of drawing the complete flag with a ruler, as we saw in the tree in figure 163. It shows self-protection certainly, and a desire to draw it correctly, but also tension because of this circumstance.

Below in figure 207 you have another example of tension in the rigid mountain scene (also drawn with the help of a ruler) by a 9 year-old girl who was never certain how her unpredictable, and often angry father would react to any situation. The sun is present but the rays have an aggressive "attitude" accompanied by dark storm clouds.

The black peaks on the mountains, rather than the usual white ones, may be an expression of disillusionment, because mountains represent goals and we climb to reach our goals, don't we? She is trying to say "what's the use?"

Figure 207

Next, in figure 208, you can literally see the anger created by and erupting from, the tension present in the scribbled drawing of a third grader.

If you follow the strokes you'll see how it starts with light pressure, then deteriorates into heavier strokes and the large spiral. He then scribbles and draws the concentric spirals. Finally he slashes out of the freehand double-spiral on the lower left and makes jab marks in the center of the scribble, declaring he wants to hit somebody. Centering spirals are never comfortable, and usually make one feel trapped. Try drawing one. *Expanding* spirals that start in the center have the effect of growing and breathing.

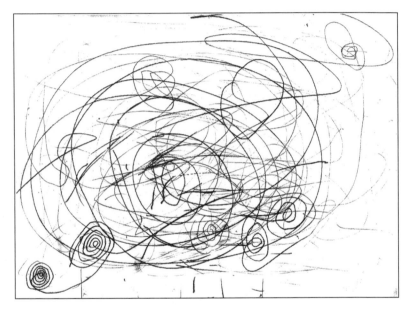

Figure 208

The confined encapsulations that you see in figure 209 show some of the 6 year-old boy's misery. We can sense just looking at the drawing that there is something unhappy going on.

The child is difficult to communicate with and seems to be marking time or regressing in his skills. He will not let any one get close enough to know him.

The school staff recently discovered that the father has terminal leukemia. He has returned from treatment at the Mayo Clinic, where the family had visited him. That is quite a load for a 6 year-old, so let's see how his drawing might manifest what is going on.

The only thing he has said is that "it is people from different states inside a circle," later identified as a "pool." A pool is an analogy, commonly used by troubled children to reflect the ominous, or a confined emotion.

The drawing is done in pencil, then colored with a blue-green marker. The encapsulations on the right side are all done in bright marker. We don't know what the centers contain, but we know he is going in circles.

The encapsulated people in the "pool" have some things in common, baldness, a few prickly hairs or the triangle shape seen on the three in the upper right. No doubt, the result of chemotherapy and radiation treatment and something else he apparently noticed while there.

The small circles around the "pool" represent people, whether this shows a desire for friends or folks watching those being treated in the "pool" we do not know.

There is a ladder or a pathway almost through the center of the "pool," perhaps showing the way out. The figure on the right, covered with blue-green and red marker may represent his father. Is this the boy's version of a cure?

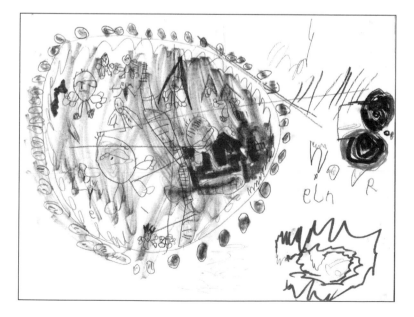

Figure 209

There are certain traits in handwriting that can be read for signals as easily as any other symbol. One of the most telling is called "the canopy." It will often be found at the end of one's name, but appears also in other words.

This stroke is always a covert plea for protection...a fear of the future, or worry over what might negatively materialize in the near future. It's as though covering the name or the word with a protective umbrella can do the same for one's trouble or fear.

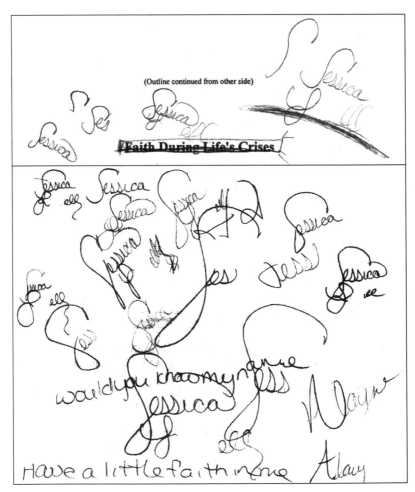

Figure 210

This stroke moves left and returns the writer to the protected past and to the mother side of the page.

A young teen, an acquaintance of one of the thirteen who died in the Columbine High School tragedy, sketched figure 210 on a church program following the shooting. Her mother said she had never seen Jessica write her name in this fashion before.

Figure 211 was part of a note written by a young newlywed, under-educated, in debt and expecting a baby.

Anyway, I just wanted to s
Mother's Day to the most
in the world.

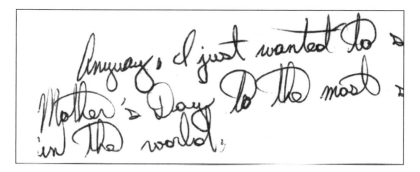

Figure 211

The note written in figure 212 shows a writer using too much space between the words. A normal expression of a need for privacy has been exaggerated into a sense of isolation and a tendency to keep a distance from others.

Vertical spaces have formed channels called "rivers," in the writing, which are clearly visible. Think of them as tears of sadness and isolation running down the page. Social communication can be a serious problem.

is still the same. So how about
those Broncos? Boy did they seem
play a good game against the Eagles. Ha Ha
Really not a whole lot going on Just
keeping ourselves to ourselves. We have
all the goodies you requested

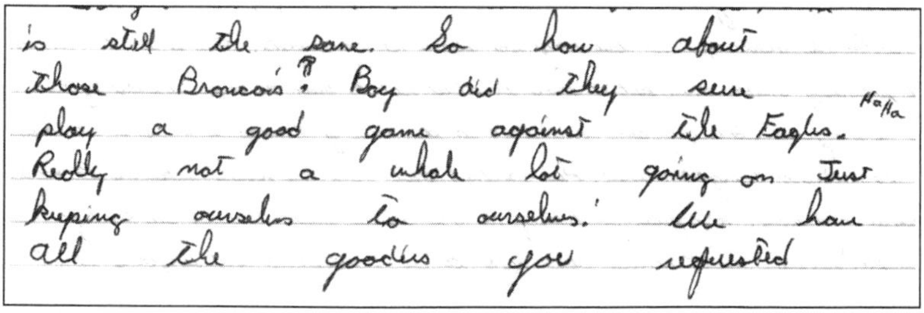

Figure 212

Satanism Or Cult Activity

This subject must be included, but the chance of touching on an actual incident is, for all practical purposes, nil. Why include it? Because it is out there. Because belief by the naïve or the uninformed that they may be exposed to satanic influence can reek havoc, if only mentally.

You know that teens especially, thrive on shocking their elders in a variety of ways. Gothic dress and cult behavior finds its way in and out of society over the years as each generation rediscovers how agitating it can be. I once used, to selfish adult advantage, profuse appreciation and admiration of a young teen who demanded to be known as "Damien." I complimented all...hair dye, skull jewelry, and Goth outfits. He was close to the end of the cycle, anyway.

Should a situation progress beyond that of startling dress, and a community discovers animal mutilations or mysterious signage don't hesitate to contact the authorities.

When suspicious, or just in need of information, one should contact not a psychological professional, but a police professional. A call to the local station or a tug on the sleeve of a local patrolman should put you in contact easily with a well-versed detective in charge of such matters. This is the *only* person you should contact. He or she will have current knowledge of your community.

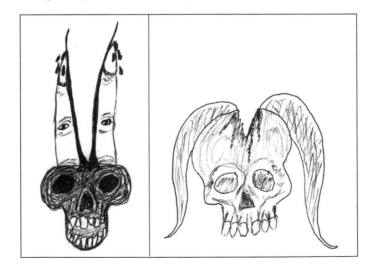

Figure 213

Figure 213 can be either a kid experimenting with grizzly drawings or a kid involved with a cult. Don't assume the worst. Shock value is a hoot for some. If drawings are more sinister or incorporate any or all of the following signage contact police; get some intervention. Again, there will have been noticeable attitude and personality changes.

Either signal in figure 214 is the cult signage indicating a black mass will take place.

Figure 214

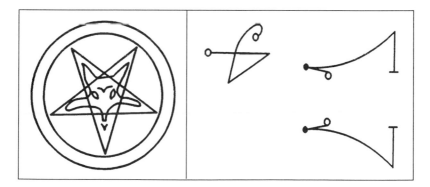

Figure 215

Figure 215 shows on the left, the baphomet, a goat head inside an inverted pentagram within a double circle and on the right, directional markers to a location.

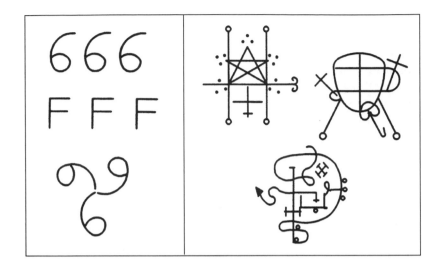

Figure 216

In figure 216 on the left are various ways to form the "mark of the devil," 666. On the right are symbols for lesser demons. There are others with a similar appearance.

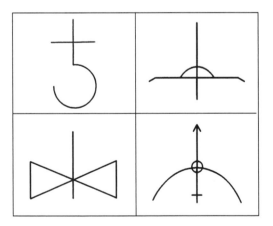

Figure 217

In figure 217 are samples of satanic symbols. Upper left is The Cross of Confusion dating from ancient times, questioning the validity of Christianity. On the lower left is

Anti-Justice, an inverted double-bladed axe. Upper right is known as Satanic Traitor, used in revenge and death threats. On the lower right is a symbol used to identify a location designated for sexual ritual.

If traces of candle wax, salt, blood, or other bizarre elements show up in closets or on clothing, or if the individual displays aggressive behavior, in addition to demonstrating a great deal of knowledge regarding rituals and has dark reading material, don't hesitate to seek help.

Games of fantasy, heavy metal music and tattooing are not cause for alarm.

Figure 218

The written spiral, winding inward, such as we see in figure 218, should offer a clue to a parent or a teacher of the writer's distress. An inward-turning spiral, as we've already mentioned, is a signal of tightly coiling stress. The center words of the spiral have been erased. The teen responsible for this was involved in a cult and suicidal.

To learn more about any type of cult consult your favorite bookseller. There are many reference sources and life-experience stories, unbelievable though they may seem, to draw from. There is no harm in educating yourself.

This has been an unpleasant chapter. We will cover one sadly appropriated symbol then move on with pleasure.

No doubt, the swastika has been the most altered symbol of this century.

Confusion reigns for some people when they see it displayed in the works of ancient cultures, in Native American art and on the chest and in the footprint of The Buddha. Indeed, it has, through the centuries, represented dynamic movement of cosmic energy and the cycle of all existence, in every way a positive.

A universal and prehistoric symbol, the cross and the circle are combined to form the solar wheel. The arms have been opened commonly toward the left, though some cultures have shown it facing both directions.

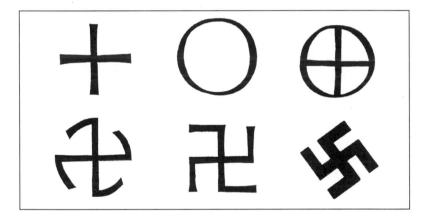

Figure 219

You can see a progression of sorts in figure 219. Though the symbol predates Christianity it was used as a disguised cross, by breaking the circumference of the circle (shown lower left), during the persecution of the Christians.

The four open arms symbolize the clockwise rotation of the solar wheel in harmony with nature; the four winds, the four seasons, the four elements (water, earth, wind, fire) and the four cardinal points (north, east, south, west).

The swastika, which means "well-being" in Sanskrit, had been used as an emblem of Aryan "purity" well before the confiscation by Hitler in 1920. He reversed the symbol, angled it to stand defiantly on one of the arms, placed it on the Nazi party banner and ground his way into history.

Chapter Nine
Let's Put It All Together

*"I will never understand children. I never pretended to.
I meet mothers all the time who make resolutions to themselves...
'I'm going to...go out of my way to show them I am interested
in them and what they do." These women end up making
rag rugs, using blunt scissors."*
Erma Bombeck

After so many examples of just what can happen on a page, we come to the fun part of combining it all. Bear in mind as you look at each picture that you are seeing it for the first time and you know nothing about it.

We have tucked a lot of knowledge into a rather small amount of space, so don't be discouraged in any way if you miss things as you look at and begin to read these drawings. You have not had the luxury of living with them for a few days, as recommended, nor do you know anything about the artist.

This section also allows an explanation regarding background coloring, which has only been touched on in its extreme, as a crosshatched encapsulation. Some drawings have been angled in order to allow the maximum size.

Where to start when deciphering a drawing? Look at the complete drawing to get a sense of the strokes, the pressure and the placement. Look for what occupies the center and what, if anything, is dominant in the picture. Then examine the rest of the content. Feel your own impressions before reading the text for each sketch.

It may take time for you to blend the signals into a sensible analysis. Be flexible with the "application" of the symbol. For instance, you understand the meaning of a bird, the meaning of a nest, and the meaning of a damaged branch. You must still fit the symbols together to glean a logical reference for, or by, the artist. The location in which a symbol appears can often make it all clear.

Most of all, have fun with your newly developed ability to peek into a drawing. You can decode a complex attitude or fathom the fleeting snapshot of a thought.

Figure 220, Girl, Age 8

The artist stands by her mother who is remarried to the man at the left, and is holding their new baby. To the far right is her new stepsister who is six months younger. The family has recently moved to a new location.

The feel of the picture, drawn in ballpoint pen, is pleasant. Parental love is reflected by the large sun, which also serves as balance for the picture.

Those large raised arms are meant as a friendly gesture, undoubtedly related to the process of trying to get acquainted and adjust, which is the theme of the sketch.

Drop your eyes to the bottom of the sketch and note the ground line, drawn after the figures were made. Her mother is extremely grounded but our artist is the only one in "free float," even after adding the line. She will not make friends as easily as the others.

She shows herself and mom with circular fingers while those of the dad and especially the sister show some aggression, though not serious. Mom is decidedly feminine and loved, with ringlets. Dad's legs are long and begin at the waist, a common expression at her age, thought to portray his being in charge. The four buttons she placed on his shirt probably reflect *their* dependence on him.

Heavily decorated skirts can show feminine identity anxiety, or in some cases impulsive or compulsive behavior. The circle pattern repeated on her skirt and Mom's shows her desire to have new friends for each of them. On close examination, the diamond pattern on the mother's skirt is actually an X pattern, which when accompanied by the heart over the pelvis, indicates her concern about being female. Her own skirt shows a prominent "wish" star. The flirtatious, loopy swirls crave excitement. She has hurriedly copied the same design on her sister's skirt.

The crown of the tree shows the energy of the foliage directed outward, which is rare. She can be a little prickly, and will not hesitate to show it.

The bird in the nest shows her need to be nurtured by her mother (location on the left of the trunk). The cut limb indicates either the divorce, the remarriage and recent relocation, or perhaps all. The bird in the sky directly above the artist shows us, in this case, her desire to flee back "home," or to her devoted grandmother, whom she misses.

Figure 220

Figure 221, Girl, Age 8

The artist is a nice, bright and accommodating, only child of a single mother. Money is tight, her mother is quite private, almost reclusive, and they live in an apartment with several pets. The child is somewhat sedentary, likes books, television and movies, and is not adventuresome. This drawing demonstrates her artistic skill, but let's sneak further around the house to see how she feels.

The drawing, done in pencil and marker, is balanced using most of the paper and has good dimension, indicating that she can recognize and solve problems.

She draws a nice walkway to welcome company, yet gives us a precarious step to navigate. Mixed messages continue with the heavily shaded door, but a generous doorknob to allow entrance. The sparse tufts of grass are not only requests for comforting, but also used as decoys.

The base of the house is wobbly, showing some insecurity, and the weak walls on the right, including the erasures betray a concern for the future and suggest a lack of any overt aggression in her nature.

Her detailed roof tile is repeated on the bay windows and indicates her active imagination. Because the shapes are quite rounded, we read a desire for company or friends, echoed by the flock of birds flying toward the house. The trapezoidal shape she gives both rooflines suggests an inner struggle. Perhaps loneliness? There is no chimney.

We can't be certain if the front windows have panes or bars. The other three windows have heavy shading with the cross sections expressing a barrier to the world. She feels protected, isolated or perhaps imprisoned.

The cloud surrounding the upper level adds anxiety to the upper room with the window barrier. We must ask the artist whose room this is. If it is hers, all this enclosure indicates something hidden. Perhaps we have something as simple as messiness, but it could be more serious. If it is the room of someone else, she is worried about—or for—that person. If it is an attic room, the hidden problem casts concern over all the occupants living in the house.

Here we have a lonely, sensitive child, who shows the need for more attention and friends in her life, yet she feels some sort of obstacle socially and is insecure about her future.

Figure 221

Figure 222, Boy, Age14

This drawing came to me through a concerned teacher. The boy is a good student, a leader and extremely well liked by all who know him. His life has recently been in turmoil because of the pending divorce of his parents. He is described as very upset and resentful.

It is hard to believe that he doesn't have a thorough knowledge of art therapy, because this pencil drawing could not be more revealing. The brain does find amazing ways to convey its coded messages. This picture is a gut-wrenching statement of the predicament in which he finds himself.

He feels victimized by the actions of his parents. He represents himself as the stump in the middle, literally "cut off at the knees" by the news, as revealed in the nonplussed expression, missing the nose. The mouth has been erased from a sad down-turned attitude to this stoic one that may represent a "stiff upper lip," or perhaps, simple resentment.

Directly above him shines the sweltering sun (notice the jagged, angry lines of the rays) of parental love, between the two apparently intact trees which represent the mother on the left and the father on the right. They are more or less identical down to his reinforcement of both at the base. The emotional trunks of each one is also reinforced, as he tries to make them stronger. He draws a ground line beneath them all, trying to provide security.

The fact that he (such as he is) locates himself in the center while the two of them are placed at the edge of the paper, only partially drawn, speaks volumes. His concern is primarily for himself, which is natural, and their situation is seen as peripheral to his.

You see the emotion carried from the trunks into the crowns of the trees where it is closed off by row after row of circular foliage. If the trees were drawn in full, the circles would be complete. The layered round-and-round motion in the crown is even more self-involved than the scribbled circles of ego involvement in the crown. "Hey, you two, what about me?"

The dark knotholes or scars on both trunks carry the message of damage, probably reflecting how he feels they have damaged themselves in his eyes. They could also be related to union and procreation in his mind, and therefore may represent the damaged marriage.

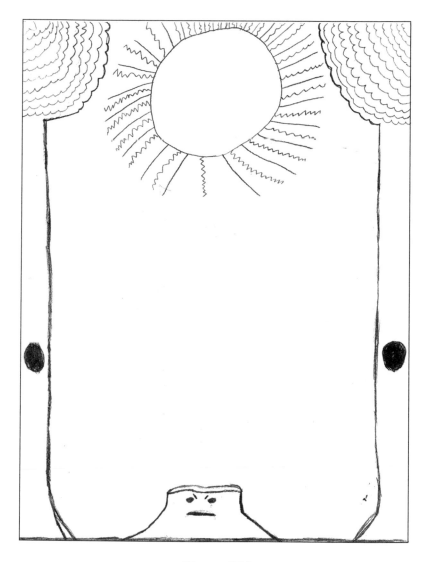

Figure 222

Figure 223, Girl, Age 7

This child has lived in many locations and situations in her short life. She is the middle daughter in a newly assembled family of five.

The significance of numbers can never be overlooked in a drawing, but she goes to great lengths with the number five. She depicts the five family members in the fruit on the tree, the five growing things in a row, (the tree, the bush, and the three flowers), and in the five separate leaves of the bush. Certain analysts might even see the three children represented as flowers or in the three sprigs of grass to the right, but yours does not.

She has two erasures in her drawing, one on the right side of the tree trunk and the other on herself in the same location. She is adjusting her place in the family, as well as in her world, and simultaneously adjusting her emotional reactions. The base of the paper is her ground line but she secures herself further with the shaded shoes.

Her tree trunk tells us, by the left side, that the natural mother is apparently weak, and we know she is absent from the little girl's life. The crown stresses the father side by its fullness and its added branch or foliage. The trunk runs well into the crown, announcing the fact that her thinking is ruled by her emotions.

She places herself on the assertive right side of the picture and the strong chin, drawn without a neck, shows some stubbornness. The repeated open-flower motif indicates she has a large capacity for love. She has chosen to use dimpling and dotting by the selection of oranges on the tree and the use of sunflowers. Often, many dots will indicate a sense of intimidation or the inability to express what one is feeling, which can be reflected in behavior as *shyness*. Those who draw tulips seem to have a sense of honesty and a measure of eloquence surrounding them.

Her short skirt announces she has an outgoing personality with nothing to hide, and the perky hat with the flower and the nicely-drawn, feminine hair all combine to show her flirtatious, but subtle, need for attention.

She is a charmer who is trying to fit into her new situation while reminding all of those around her that she is still a little bit special.

Figure 223

Let's take some time to look at some special signals in various tree drawings and compare them to facts we know about the artists.

Figure 224

This young teen from an inner city school is bright and talented. His parents are divorced. He is dealing with an increasing amount of frustration and anger in his life.

He tries to stabilize with the very wide trunk, which then opens simultaneously to the unconscious and base elements. His emotion carries far into the mental area of the closed crown. You can see the tree has divided into three dominant branches, whether these are people or areas of interest only he can say. The right angle of the tree shows he identifies with the masculine nature.

Both his mom and dad have disappointed him. The lower right branch, representing the father, has forked and is dead in one area. Its upper fork is the least significant on the tree and in the process of disappearing into the future.

The mother branch on the lower left has turned down, but he offers a peephole into the foliage as though trying to understand her. The other branches, which can represent stronger aspects of his mother or other female relatives, sustain the foliage of the partially closed crown.

What appears to be a nest at the upper right looks more like a soccer ball in the original. Any object placed on a branch reinforces it. In this instance it represents a future aspiration of his. The pincer-like branch on the top left of the crown has cruelly snared a kite, showing a major disappointment regarding one of his prior goals or dreams.

Figure 225

The eighth grade boy who drew figure 225 seems to have it all. He comes from a successful and wealthy family.

He is handsome, competitive, catered to by all, and has an enthusiasm for life that spreads to those around him.

You see the enthusiasm immediately by the clear flow of emotion from the open base, through the trunk to the open crown of his tree which is spreading off the page at the top, as well as both sides.

In what may be an act of compassion or generosity, as he is "vertically challenged," he dangles the 14 (his exact age) apples on the bottom branch within the reach of all.

Figure 226

The tree in figure 226 fills the page, yet it is not grounded, even by the bottom of the page, leaving a large area wide open to unconscious influences and basic drives.

You may recognize the "A-bomb" appearance of the sentimentally self-indulgent wide trunk and full crown. You see that the crown is closed to the environment, but almost completely open to the trunk. There are no squiggles, swirls or signs of foliage in the crown. With all of these instincts feeding the abundance of emotion in the trunk, and the lack of mental activity in the crown, you can be sure this teenager is self serving and rather shallow.

The sharp pointed branches entering the crown—like so many knives—show emotion being brought into the mental approach in a cutting, piercing fashion straight from the instinctual sphere. Life will be viewed as a competition and unless things change, this child will not hesitate to say or do what is deemed necessary in order to win.

Figure 227

I was sorry to see this tree in figure 227, and especially sorry to learn it was drawn by a high school girl. Perhaps you too, can feel the testy emotion of it before understanding why.

The tree itself goes off the paper at the three sides. This is not a demonstration of enthusiasm but of "edging." Edging is found often in drawings of older people who may use it to signal a lack of vitality, or that their life is moving toward the end, when the drawing occupies the right edge of the paper. It is not necessarily done with a tree, but any kind of scenery confined to only the edge or edges of the paper. It could also be used by someone who wants to remain "out of the spotlight," and when asked to draw a tree, may draw several at one confined edge of the paper.

But the artist of this tree is accustomed to being a bystander, one of those who never occupy center stage in life. This is not to say that she is recalcitrant or mousy, but really quite the opposite. She will be an imposing presence, she may even be a large girl, and will make her thoughts and opinions known.

The busy and interlaced branches (showing some confusion in her thinking) comprising the crown show the mental activity, but look at those shaded, wedge-shaped "claws" all throughout, even in the crotch of the crown where the other main branch of the tree angles away. Any symbol showing up in the crown will relate somehow to its basic meaning. In this case, claws show a clutching tenacity in grasping and holding on to knowledge, ideas and—most certainly—opinions. The pointed branches seem to puncture the environment, so she and her attitude cannot be received well by others.

She draws long lines of defensive bark on the trunk, which we assume is wider at the base than shown. There is no doubt her emotional responses show up directly in her thinking patterns, because the crown is completely open. The knothole appears to be closing, therefore healing, if it refers to a specific trauma.

Her pathway occupies the lower center of the page and winds toward the left in the distance with no apparent destination. She is nursing some old hurts and dwelling in the past. The dotting on the pathway shows some form of intimidation or nervousness, while the sparse tufts of grass (reflecting her age) along the sides indicate she could use some nurturing, in spite of herself. The slashed markings on the ground, as well as on the path, betray her extreme impatience.

Figure 228

The teenage boy responsible for this smudged pencil sketch in figure 228 is described as something of a nerd, a nonproductive person, yet bright.

The extremely light pressure indicates the take-it-or-leave-it attitude along with feelings of deserving more than he has, as the tree is drawn on the wide axis of the page.

You can see by the modest size of the trunk that he invests little emotion into his surroundings, but does carry emotion far into his thinking patterns, that is until it is closed off by the small puffs of unimaginative foliage.

The crown splits into three main branches and then others, covered by those small clumps of foliage. Therein lies his problem. His interests are so numerous and so varied that he feels inundated by "stuff," yet his energy and attention are so limited that he is able to pursue very little.

When interests, people or opportunity phase out of his life, he probably views it as a relief. He may care in his limited way, but the easy way out will triumph.

Figure 229, Boy, Age 7

Here we have a family drawing, done in marker, by the young boy with the worm. He is the youngest child in the family and places himself where he feels the most comfortable, between his parents. It was drawn at school and the teacher titled the figures. His brother is two years his senior. His sister is approximately fourteen.

He draws his mother as the only one with feet and more firmly grounded at the bottom of the page than the rest of the family. He still utilizes the triangle dress to depict the mature female, and none of his figures have a neck. Also missing are the ears, but his drawing in general is not advanced so this all holds no particular meaning.

Hands are missing on the sister, but portrayed as gentle on the mother. The interesting ones are those on all three of the males, done as boxing gloves. There is a lot of rough housing and wrestling done in fun among them, and it may be the primary way they show affection. He feels his older brother picks on him routinely (not unusual), which may be the reason he is portrayed totally in black. Notice that his father has a black belt, which may be interpreted that he is unbeatable.

His father is portrayed as very tall even though in reality he is the same height as the mother, so the boy conveys that Dad is important to him, and apparently in charge. We see again how strongly he identifies with Dad, because he touches him in two places in the drawing.

The most interesting thing in the drawing is the encapsulation of the sister and her missing hands. She is in her teens and intolerant, of course, of her younger brothers, which could be reason enough for him to wall her off. In their case though, the two had innocently been playing a physical game in which he ended up with a broken arm. She routinely teases in a joking way, that she can do it to him again. He takes no chances.

Why the worm? Most young boys are fascinated with them as well as other critters, aren't they? But this family also lives in a tropical area where pinworms are prevalent among young children who are notoriously fond of playing in dirt. He appears to be acknowledging the problem.

I repeat. Know the artist and the circumstances.

Figure 229

Figure 230, Girl, Age 5-6

This cute drawing was not dated so the best guess of the little girl, now 10 years-old, and her mother is that it was done around the age of five or six.

The theme of the drawing is easy to see. There had been horses included in the routine of the little girl's family for years before her birth, and she obviously has a horse or horses on her mind. She is either hoping for one of her own, or looking forward to her next riding lesson. There is a "whee" (spelled differently) included in the "thought picture" over her head, not easily seen.

As we've discussed before, a child this age is still drawing a rather large head, and it is the first aspect drawn. The neck, shoulder and body all appear to be one, as is still common with some at this age. Her eyes are small slits showing that she is self-absorbed, and not overly interested in investigating things outside of her own domain. She has no ears but may not routinely draw them yet. She has given herself a nice amount of hair, showing a good acceptance of her own brain power or intelligence.

She continues the body proportionately until she runs out of paper. This is not, in any way, a drawing that stops at the waist, for any other reason. The very sturdy hands and arms are made to serve her well. A girl has to hang on to a horse, after all. She feels capable.

Her background is in one color, not heavily cross-hatched indicating the isolation of a minor encapsulation, as we saw back in figure 93, but drawn with just enough attention to advise others to kindly keep their distance. You may consider this, any time you see it, as an indication of shyness in the child. In this case the extremely small eyes, and perhaps the missing ears, echo her shyness.

To explain further, the background is lightly colored and the strokes go in a horizontal direction at the top, then in a vertical direction behind the figure and horizontally again in the lower area. All quite orderly, rather than scrawled in random directions, as a crosshatch would be. This is an effort to keep elbow room in her own space, rather than a sense of isolation. This translates to shyness.

This particular little artist was extremely, almost painfully, shy for this period of time in her life and is now blossoming nicely.

Figure 230

Figure 231, Girl, Age 8

As you remember, the subject of any drawing which is the same sex and age as the sketcher and not otherwise identified, is the artist.

This was done in black ballpoint and colored with markers. The dress is a bright green and the wings are dotted with pastels. Nothing else is colored. Dark items are shaded in ballpoint.

There is a clutching aggression in the pointed shape of the fingers and sleeves, also reflected in the wingtips and tail of the bird. Her abundant hair is heavily shaded and she has drawn a well-formed neck and shoulder line, which is not routinely included at this age. These are signals that she feels she is intelligent and is accepting of her body and physicality. She might even feel superior to her age group.

The entire feel of the sketch is one of a girl in the clutches of dark, crawly insects but reaching for the light flying bird and butterfly, symbolizing a sense of freedom, as well as transformation. The spider, considered ominous, is weaving a web in her wings, which constrains her own free movement. The caterpillar is attached to her hem, and both seem intent on holding her back.

This figure was provided by her grandmother and drawn five years prior to her sketch of the tree in figure 188. You might take a moment to reread that explanation of her bipolar condition.

She had drawn irises in her eyes, then shaded over them, which is difficult to see in the reproduction. This represents an unwillingness to see things as they are.

These are sad little legs and feet. She tries to add strength to the convoluted legs by shading them. This adds, unfortunately, to the immobility of the figure. The heavy embossing can be seen and felt through the paper. And a most important point—the weak small feet are standing on *tiptoe!* You may not remember the reference, but any figure standing on tiptoes is an obvious, curious and extremely rare, portrayal of having a tenuous grasp on reality. Neither the drawing nor the figure is grounded in any way.

The drawing seems to be saying that she is aware of—and caught up in—two very different expressions of her nature and she seeks the lighter and freer side of herself.

Figure 231

Figure 232, Boy, Age 7

This artist is the younger brother of the girl who did such a nice job on the trees and leaves in figure 182. You can see a similarity, in part because they spend so much time together at the art table. Content is the same in parts of the pictures, such as clouds, birds, the sun, grass and flowers, but he puts his own signature on the style used to draw them. Their greatest similarity is in the butterflies and the fullness of the drawings. He too, has a balance of numbers, but not to the degree of his sister.

He has one theme—and only one—in this pencil drawing. The puppy. So small, how can this be the subject? The puppy occupies the center, if not the middle of the drawing, but the dead giveaway is the secure, heavy leash. Would you say he does not want this little guy to get away? He shows the puppy being walked, tended and no doubt, guarded, by a responsible mature woman, wearing high heels and carrying a purse.

Because he is not in the picture, we can assume that he doesn't have a puppy, but desperately wants one. His mother vigorously confirmed this when I asked. A puppy is in the future plans, when he is a little older.

He draws a two level house with the door wide open and a watermelon generously ready for sharing on the table. He wanted to add more fruit, but ran out of time.

Remember what we know about an open door...the artist needs social contact and approval from others. A window in the door enforces the need for contact, and he has drawn a large one. He shows a doorknob and at the bottom of the door look what we have—a doggie door.

He draws his tree over on the masculine side of the page and shows a wide open crown. He uses the flowers in the tree like leaves, to filter the outside influence of others, as though he realizes that he is very anxious to please, and may need to protect his own thoughts and ideas.

The slender trunk has very lightly drawn bark for a bit of protection. It is unusual for a youngster to have such an open crown, so I suspect this child is very sensitive to not only his own emotional reactions, but also to those of others. His swirled skyline reveals a tendency to worry.

The future puppy will be one very lucky little critter to have such a sensitive and caring master.

Figure 232

Figure 233, Boy, age 14

This, to me, is a charming picture, now that I know the circumstances under which it was drawn.

What do we see? An intricately drawn fence with a gate, showing the hinges on the left and the clasp on the right. Well-drawn lights on the gate posts. He not only has some artistic talent, but willingly detailed the nail heads and slats of the fence. All the effort concentrated at the bottom of the drawing with no tangible theme, and nothing drawn in the important center of the page. The gate has to lead somewhere, we say, doesn't it? What is putting him off so completely that he cannot sketch anything further into the drawing? Why bother to start such a picture? And what's with the hole on the right side? We can tell that he drew the flimsy grass at the bottom first, then worked the fence into it using heavy pressure.

What do we know regarding such fences and gates? Fences indicate the occupant needs and wants protection. Wait a minute, when there is a gate, the artist may want a change of his situation. He may feel the need to escape.

I would be absolutely puzzled and confounded if I didn't know the circumstances under which a picture like this was drawn, and certainly would not try to interpret the drawing, as we discussed early on in these pages.

Could an analyst, anxious to interpret, make a case for an unhappy teen trying to break out of an oppressive circumstance, probably within the family? Maybe, but with no house to indicate that, how could one know? And why would an analyst go out on that precarious limb?

The middle school teacher who gave me this had grown fond of her class and was sending them on to high school. Being a middle-age nester herself, she asked them to draw what their home and family would be like ten years from that day. The results were predictable for assigned drawings...from castles to cardboard boxes!

This boy, a recent immigrant from a harsh life in Europe, and speaking little English, was asked to commit to a responsibility in the following decade! Now we can see and understand the "Don't fence me in...lemme outa here" message. This drawing has a complete honesty. The light grounding is understandable, as is the heavy pressure while he stalled by drawing the fence. The hole—is priceless.

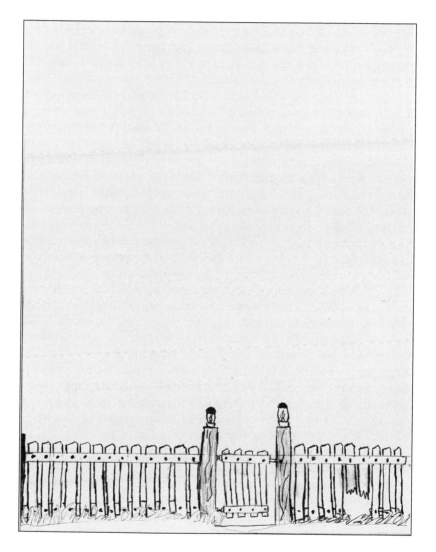

Figure 233

Are you pleased with how much you can now see in what appears to be only refrigerator art? Your ability will increase as you use it and continue to investigate further. The following bibliography contains a beginning reading list for you and each book has its own further list of references. I know of only one situation in which an individual seemed to have learned too much about a particular subject...

...a friend of mine, a graphologist and elementary school teacher, delights in telling of the little boy who complained that his class assignment provided "more about penguins than I want to know."

Our web site is www.signalsfromthechild.com where we will continue to explore the drawings of children and adolescents, as well as venturing into "doodles" involving various ages. I invite you to visit and sign up, if you are interested, for the free online newsletter. Some of you may also want to send a drawing for a possible online analysis. You will find the particulars for this free service at the web site.

While I am eager and pleased to receive interesting drawings, please don't send them to me without including your permission to use them, even though the sketch will remain anonymous if it is used in the future in any manner. A standard permission form is available on the web site, but a copy is also included in the back of this book for your convenience. Any information you can send with a drawing concerning the artist or the circumstances of a sketch is welcome, and as you have read, may be necessary in order to unlock the complete meaning.

Remember to keep an open mind, to analyze with a generous attitude, and to always consider all aspects of the symbols present in any drawing. Never be hasty; allow time for a sketch to speak to you.

I look forward to hearing from you either at the web site or through the publisher's address.

Bibliography

Amend, Karen & **Ruiz**, Mary, *Handwriting Analysis,* Van Nuys, Ca: Newcastle Publishing, 1980

Bach, Susan, *Life Paints Its Own Span,* Einsiedeln, Switzerland, Daimon Verlag, 1990

Bolander, Karen, *Assessing Personality Through Tree Drawings,* New York: Basic Books, Inc., 1977.

Bruce-Mitford, Miranda, *The Illustrated Book of Signs & Symbols,* New York: DK Books, 1996.

Buck, John N., *The House-Tree-Person Technique, Revised manual.* Los Angeles: Western Psychological Services, 1966.

Burns, Robert C., *Kinetic-House-Tree-Person Drawings,* New York: Brunner/Mazel, 1987.

Campbell, Joseph, *The Hero With A Thousand Faces,* Princeton: Princeton University Press, 1972.

Campbell, Joseph, *The Power Of Myth,* New York: Doubleday, 1988.

Capacchione, Lucia, *The Power of Your Other Hand,* Van Nuys, Ca: Newcastle Publishing, 1988

Capacchione, Lucia, *The Picture of Health,* Carson, Ca: Hay House, Inc., 1990.

Circlot, J.E., *A Dictionary Of Symbols,* London: Routledge & Kegan Paul, 1971.

Coles, Robert, *The Spiritual Life of Children.* Boston, Ma: Houghton Mifflin, 1990.

Cooper, J.C., *An Illustrated Encyclopedia of Traditional Symbols,* London: Routledge & Kegan Paul, 1962.

Cox, Maureen, *Children's Drawings,* London: Penguin Books, 1992.

DiLeo, Joseph H., *Young Children and Their Drawings,* New York: Brunner/Mazel, 1970.

DiLeo, Joseph H., *Interpreting Children's Drawings,* New York: Brunner/Mazel, 1983.

Jung, Carl G., *Man And His Symbols,* New York; Dell, 1960.

Edwards, Betty, *Drawing on the Right Side of the Brain,* Los Angeles: J.P. Tarcher, Inc., 1979.

Edwards, Betty, *Drawing on the Artist Within,* New York: Simon & Schuster, Inc., 1987

Fincher, Susanne F., *Creating Mandalas*, Boston, Ma: Shambala Publications, Inc., 1991.

Furth, Gregg M., *The Secret World Of Drawings*, Boston: Sigo Press, 1988.

Gardner, Howard, *Artful Scribbles*, New York: Basic Books, Inc., 1980.

Hartford, Huntington, *You Are What You Write*, New York: Macmillan Publishing, 1973

Kellogg, Rhoda, *Analyzing Children's Art*, Palo Alto, Ca: Mayfield Publishing Co., 1969.

Kellogg, Rhoda, *Children's Drawings/Children's Minds*, New York: Avon Books, 1979.

Klepsch, Marvin & Logie, Laura, *Children Draw and Tell*, New York; Brunner/Mazel, 1982

Koppitz, E.M., *Psychological Evaluation of Children's Human Figure Drawings*, Orlando, Fl: Grune & Stratton, Inc., 1968.

Kramer, Edith, *Art as Therapy with Children.*, New York: Schocken Books, Inc., 1977.

Levick, Myra, *See What I'm Saying*, Dubuque, Ia: Islewest Publishing, 1998.

Machover, Karen, *Personality Projection in the Drawing of the Human Figure*, Springfield, Il: Charles C. Thomas, 1949.

Malchiodi, Cathy, *Understanding Children's Drawings*, New York: Guilford Press, 1998.

Malchiodi, Cathy, *Breaking the Silence: Art therapy With Children From Violent Homes (sec .ed. rev.)*, New York: Brunner/Mazel, 1997.

Mendel, Alfred O., *Personality in Handwriting (reprint)*, Van Nuys, Ca: Newcastle Publishing, 1990.

Olyanova, Nadya, *Handwriting Tells*, North Hollywood, Ca., Wilshire Book, 1973.

Roman, Klara, *Handwriting, A Key to Personality*, New York: Pantheon Books, 1952.

Siegel, Bernie, *Love, Medicine and Miracles*, New York: Harper & Row, 1986.

Solomon, Shirl, *Knowing Your Child Through His Handwriting and Drawings* ,New York, Crown, 1978.

Tresidder, Jack, *Dictionary of Symbols*, San Francisco: Chronicle Books, 1988.

Wadeson, Harriet, *Art Psychotherapy*, New York: John Wiley & Sons, 1980.

Index

A

abuse, 54, 221-235
activity, 74, 194
Adam and Eve, 153
adolescence, 45
adolescent, 65, 81, 133
  and drawing, 81
aggression, 98
airplane, 208
angel, 208
animals, 209
anxiety 13,
apple, 209
approach to an interpretation, 22
apron, 209
arms, 139, 140, 248
  raised, 46, 248
  size and condition, 139
arrow, 205
art therapists, 221
artist, 47
  in the drawing, 47
assigned pictures, 19
axis of the paper
  horizontal or vertical, 200

B

Bach, Susan R., 83
background coloring, 247, 264
bag, 209
balance, 36, 39, 46, 53, 66
ball, 209
balloon, 209
bark, 188, 260, 268
base of the tree, 181, 184. See
  root

basket, 209
bell, 209
belly button, 209
belt, 209
bipolar disorder, 202, 266
bird, 195, 248
  nest or eggs, 195
birdhouse, 195
birds, 194, 209, 250
boats and water, 121, 209
body
  three sections of, 135
body image, 100-105
Bolander, Dr. Karen, 154, 185
book, 210
boots, 210
bottle, 210
bows, 210
box, 205
box-shaped body, 50, 67
  See square body.
branch, 162, 256
branches, 158, 191, 257
  covering the trunk, 165
  divided, 256
  healthy or damaged, 189
  interlaced, claw-shaped, 260
  sharp, 259
breasts, 210
bridge, 210
Buddha, 153
buds, 166, 192
bulge,
  in tree trunk, 177
bull, 210
butterfly, 210
buttons, 51, 69, 98, 210

Permission To Reprint Material

Jean Coles has my permission to use the accompanying drawing in any and all forms. This could include electronic and/or printed forms, advertising and promotions, as well as any derivative or subsidiary works, including book clubs and special editions, articles, tapes, and other languages, nonexclusively throughout the world.

The drawing is best described as follows:

_____

_____

_____

Artist and circumstance:

_____

_____

_____

(The name will never be used to identify the material. You may describe the relationship, age, and some things known about the artist that might relate to the drawing.)

I am the owner of, or in position to grant permission for the use of this material.

_____   _____
Signature   Date

"Do not go where the path may lead,
go instead where there is no
path and leave a trail."
Emerson

About The Author

What of interest can be learned in a half page?

Denver is home, though Jean Coles spent many years living out of the country. She attended University of Colorado at Denver, has been certified by the International Graphoanalysis Society and has three children who are wonderful citizens.

She proudly cast her first vote for JFK, considered the Women's Lib movement redundant, and learned to play golf in the winter rain of Buenos Aires with the Belgian Chargé's wife, who swore marvelously in Spanish.

She has skied Alaskan mountaintops, peered into Costa Rican volcanoes, and retrieved a lost three year-old in Rio de Janeiro. She's swum with sea snakes and in Liberian undertows, but so far, has successfully avoided crossing the Continental Divide on horseback with her husband.

Jean is shocked at how fond she is of her own nine grandchildren, in addition to her husband's four, and has never ridden a bicycle.

Your personal information will never be shared. Ever.

Order Form

Check your local bookstore or quickly order here

Call: **800-690-EMBA (3622)** toll free
Have credit card ready.
or
Order from web site:
wwwsignalsfromthechild.com
or
Send a copy of this form with payment to: EMBA House,
P.O.Box 100891, Denver, Colorado, 80250.

Yes, send ____ copies of **Signals From The Child**:
Learn to read the secrets in drawings and refrigerator art at
$19.95 each. (Colorado residents, please add $1.40 sales
tax per book.)

Add $4 U.S. priority shipping for first book, and $2
each additional book. (International orders must be
accompanied by postal money order in U.S. funds, please,
and add $9 shipping, $5 each additional book.)

For large quantities, contact publisher for discount.

Name_____

Address_____

City_____St._____Zip_____

e-mail_____Ph:_____

My check or money order for $_____ is enclosed.

Please charge my credit card:
Visa_____ Mastercard_____ Discover_____ Am. Express_____

Name on card _____

Card Number_____Exp.Date___/___

Your personal information will never be shared. Ever.

Order Form

Check your local bookstore or quickly order here

Call: **800-690-EMBA (3622)** toll free
Have credit card ready.
or
Order from web site:
wwwsignalsfromthechild.com
or
Send a copy of this form with payment to: EMBA House,
P.O.Box 100891, Denver, Colorado, 80250.

Yes, send _____ copies of **Signals From The Child**: *Learn to read the secrets in drawings and refrigerator art* at $19.95 each. (Colorado residents, please add $1.40 sales tax per book.)

Add $4 U.S. priority shipping for first book, and $2 each additional book. (International orders must be accompanied by postal money order in U.S. funds, please, and add $9 shipping, $5 each additional book.)

For large quantities, contact publisher for discount.

Name_____

Address_____

City_____St._____Zip_____

e-mail_____Ph:_____

My check or money order for $_____ is enclosed.

Please charge my credit card:
Visa_____ Mastercard_____ Discover_____ Am. Express_____

Name on card _____

Card Number_____Exp.Date___/___

Your personal information will never be shared. Ever.

Order Form

Check your local bookstore or quickly order here

Call: **800-690-EMBA (3622)** toll free
Have credit card ready.
or
Order from web site:
wwwsignalsfromthechild.com
or
Send a copy of this form with payment to: EMBA House,
P.O.Box 100891, Denver, Colorado, 80250.

Yes, send ____ copies of **Signals From The Child**: *Learn to read the secrets in drawings and refrigerator art* at $19.95 each. (Colorado residents, please add $1.40 sales tax per book.)

Add $4 U.S. priority shipping for first book, and $2 each additional book. (International orders must be accompanied by postal money order in U.S. funds, please, and add $9 shipping, $5 each additional book.)

For large quantities, contact publisher for discount.

Name_____

Address_____

City_____St._____Zip_____

e-mail_____Ph:_____

My check or money order for $_____ is enclosed.

Please charge my credit card:
Visa____ Mastercard____ Discover____ Am. Express____

Name on card _____

Card Number_____Exp.Date___/__